Robert K. Cooper

THE
CONSCIENCE
OF AN AGNOSTIC

TABLE OF CONTENTS

INTRODUCTION

Throughout history, the subject of religion has been a source of unending controversy. Dating back to ancient Greece's polytheistic religious systems right up until the present day, there have been numerous believers in one or more deities. These believers have represented many different religious affiliations; Christianity, Judaism, Buddhism, Hinduism, and Islam being the most popular. There have also been many atheists, agnostics, deists, and pantheists, some of whom were quite brilliant. In the appendix of this book, I've provided a list of agnostics who have made significant contributions to the advancement of civilization in the fields of science, art, literature, and other areas of human endeavor. It seems rather strange that a God would allow such widespread disagreement among believers and skeptics over a subject of such paramount importance. Instead, I would expect that the vast majority of reasonably intelligent people would either be believers or doubters, with just a small minority holding an opposing viewpoint. From a personal standpoint, I'm not at all happy about being agnostic. I would much rather be a devout Christian or a devoted member of some other religious tradition. However, I feel that I cannot do violence to my conscience by lying to myself. Thus, to be intellectually honest with myself and others, I must be content to remain agnostic unless I have a significant revelation at some point.

CHAPTER 1

What is Agnosticism?

Agnosticism is the belief that the existence of a God, in the sense of a supernatural being, is entirely unknowable. Agnosticism contends that it can neither be proven nor disproven whether there is a God or Gods because it is beyond the human mind's capacity to make this determination. An agnostic might also be an individual who professes neither of two opposing positions on a particular subject. The word *agnostic* means "without knowledge."

The earliest professed agnostic was the Greek philosopher Protagoras, who originally came from the city of Thrace in northern Greece and later established himself as a teacher and advisor in Athens. He was considered by Plato to be a sophist, a specific type of teacher in ancient Greece during the fourth and fifth centuries BC. Some sophists utilized the tools of philosophy and rhetoric. Others taught subjects such as music, athletics, and mathematics to young nobility.

Protagoras caused serious controversy by claiming that "man is the measure of all things," which Plato interpreted to mean that absolute truth does not exist. There is only that which individuals consider to be the truth. This idea of individual relativity was quite revolutionary at the time and stood in sharp contrast to other philosophical concepts, which argued that the universe is based on objective forces apart from human influence or perceptions.[1]

The original coining of the term *agnosticism* in the 1880s is credited to Thomas Henry Huxley, an English biologist specializing in comparative anatomy. He was sometimes referred to as "Darwin's Bulldog" due to his strong support of Charles Darwin's theory of evolution. Huxley was somewhat reluctant to accept a few of Darwin's ideas, such as gradualism and natural selection, but he was unwavering in his public support of Darwin. Huxley played a central role in the spread of scientific education in Great Britain and was opposed to the more extreme versions of religious tradition. He is quoted as stating, "Agnosticism, in fact, is not a creed, but a method, the essence of which lies in the rigorous application of a single principle...the fundamental axiom of modern science...In matters of the intellect, follow your reason as far as it will take you, without regard to any other consideration...In matters of the intellect, do not pretend that conclusions are certain which are not demonstrated or demonstrable."[2]

There are several different types of agnosticism that will be briefly explained here:

1) Strong Agnosticism - This point of view is called hard agnosticism, closed agnosticism, strict agnosticism, absolute agnosticism, or epistemological agnosticism. It contends that the existence or non-existence of a God or Gods cannot be known due to men's inability to confirm any

experience with anything other than another subjective experience.

2) Mild Agnosticism - This perspective is known as weak agnosticism, soft agnosticism, open agnosticism, empirical agnosticism, or temporal agnosticism. It contends that the existence or non-existence of a God or Gods is unknown at this point, but it may not be unknowable at some point. Therefore, the most logical course of action is to suspend judgment until more reliable evidence is made available.

3) Pragmatic Agnosticism - This point of view contends that one cannot know if a God or Gods exist with any degree of certainty. However, even if they do exist, they do not seem to show sufficient interest in humanity's affairs, so there is no reason to concern oneself with them.

4) Agnostic Theism - This point of view is also called religious agnosticism. An agnostic theist believes in the existence of a God or Gods but considers the basis of this proposition to be unknown or inherently unknowable.

5) Agnostic Atheism - This is the point of view that claims not to know of the existence or non-existence of a God or Gods but rejects such a possibility in the absence of any concrete, scientific evidence.

CHAPTER 2

What is Religious Faith?

The dictionary definition of faith is that it is the theological virtue defined as secure belief in God and a trusting acceptance of God's will. We can define religious faith as confidence or trust in a particular system of religious belief. For a Christian, these are not just empty words on a page but rather serve as the basis for one's entire life. Religious faith is acceptance of what we cannot perceive in a physical sense but feel deep within ourselves. Some consider it an essential element if one is to have any relationship with God. Religious faith is the assurance that those things that are revealed and promised in God's word, although we do not see them, are real and provide the believer with the conviction that what he expects to occur in faith will come to pass. Rationality depends on reason and facts that can be scientifically determined, whereas religious faith relies on inspiration or a perceived revelation. Some claim that religious faith transcends reason, and those who have it lead blessed, deeply spiritual lives despite the trials and setbacks they may encounter as they journey through this earthly existence. They consider religious faith to be a precious possession even though it is not a visible or tangible entity.

There are numerous biblical references to religious faith. Some of the most often cited verses are the following:

"For by grace you have been saved through faith. And this is not your own doing; it is the gift of God, not a result of works, so that no one may boast" (Ephesians 2:8-9).

"For we walk by faith, not by sight" (2 Corinthians 5:7).

"I have fought the good fight, I have finished the race, I have kept the faith" (2 Timothy 4:7).

"Yet we know that a person is not justified by works of the law, but through faith in Jesus Christ, so we also have believed in Christ Jesus, in order to be justified by faith in Christ and not by works of the law, because by works of the law no one will be justified" (Galatians 2:16).

"I have been crucified with Christ. It is no longer I who live, but Christ who lives in me. And the life I now live in the flesh I live by faith in the Son of God, who loved me and gave himself for me" (Galatians 2:20).

"For by the grace given to me, I say to everyone among you not to think of himself more highly than he ought to think, but to think with sober judgment, each according to the measure of faith that God has assigned" (Romans 12:3).

"If any of you lacks wisdom, let him ask God, who gives generously to all without reproach, and it will be given him. But let him ask in faith, with no doubting, for the one who doubts is like a wave of the sea that is driven and tossed by the wind. For that person must not suppose that he will receive anything from the Lord; he is a double-minded man, unstable in all his ways" (James 1:5-8).

"And whatever you ask in prayer, you will receive, if you have faith" (Matthew 21:22).

"That your faith might not rest in the wisdom of men but in the power of God" (1 Corinthians 2:5).

"And without faith, it is impossible to please him, for whoever would draw near to God must believe that he exists and that he rewards those who seek him" (Hebrews 11:6).

Many scholars throughout history have been quite skeptical regarding the concept of religious faith. They question why we should have faith in a God who allows war, disease, famine, poverty, crime, and other horrible afflictions. The philosopher Bertrand Russell stated the following regarding religious faith: "Christians hold that their faith does good, but other faiths do harm. At any rate, they hold this about the communist faith. What I wish to maintain is that *all* faiths do harm. We may define 'faith' as a firm belief in something for which there is no evidence. Where there is evidence, no one speaks of 'faith.' We do not speak of faith that two and two are four or that the earth is round. We only speak of faith when we wish to substitute emotion for evidence. The substitution of emotion for evidence is apt to lead to strife since different groups substitute different emotions. Christians have faith in the Resurrection; communists have faith in Marx's Theory of Value. Neither faith can be defended rationally, and each, therefore, is defended by propaganda and, if necessary, by war."[3]

My personal opinion on the matter is that there is no rational basis for religious faith. I have difficulty with the idea that religious faith transcends human reasoning since I don't understand how anyone can convincingly defend this position. I suppose that I could say that I have religious faith because some highly esteemed individuals proudly proclaim their reliance on it. Be that as it may, how can I be assured with a high degree of confidence that these people are not just sadly deluded or are even being deceitful with less noble goals in mind? On the other hand, I do have hope for the future in a probabilistic sense. We can take commonsense measures regarding the overall quality of our lives, including our health and safety. Nonetheless, tragedy can still blindside us at any moment without the slightest warning. However, I do not have what one would perceive as religious faith. I never have, and I doubt that I ever will.

CHAPTER 3

Common Objections to the Bible

There are some commonly voiced objections to the Bible. One of the most significant complaints involves the subject of homosexuality. There are quite a few biblical references to this subject, and some of the most frequently cited are the following:

> "Thou shalt not lie with mankind, as with womankind: it is an abomination" (Leviticus 18:22).

> "If a man has sexual relations with a man as one does with a woman, both of them have done what is detestable. They are to be put to death; their blood will be on their own heads" (Leviticus 20:13).

> "Or do you not know that the unrighteous will not inherit the kingdom of God? Do not be deceived: neither the sexually immoral, nor idolaters, nor men who practice homosexuality, nor thieves, nor the greedy, nor drunkards, nor revilers, nor swindlers will inherit the kingdom of God" (1 Corinthians 6:9-10).

"For this reason [turning away from God] God gave them up to dishonorable passions. For their women exchanged natural relations for those that are contrary to nature, and the men likewise gave up natural relations with women and were consumed with passion for one another, men committing shameless acts with men and receiving in themselves the due penalty for their error"

(Romans 1:26-27).

"The law is not laid down for the just but for the lawless and disobedient, for the ungodly and sinners, for the unholy and profane, for those who strike their fathers and mothers, for murderers, for the sexually immoral, men who practice homosexuality, enslavers, liars, perjurers, and whatever else is contrary to sound doctrine"

(1 Timothy 1:9-10).

"Even as Sodom and Gomorrah, and the cities about them in like manner, giving themselves over to fornication, and going after strange flesh, are set forth for an example, suffering the vengeance of eternal fire"

(Jude 1:7).

All of these Bible verses suggest that if a man is genuinely homosexual and has been for as long as he can remember, going back to his early childhood, then according to the Bible, he must be put to death. His execution would probably take the form of stoning since that was all the rage in those days. How is it possible that such an allegedly sacred text would endorse such barbarism?

Another common objection involves the institution of slavery in the Bible. Some maintain that the ancient practice of slavery discredits the Bible, and there are Bible verses that support this contention:

> "When a man strikes his male or female slave with a rod so hard that the slave dies under his hand, he shall be punished. If, however, the slave survives for a day or two, he is not to be punished, since the slave is his own property"
>
> (Exodus 21:20-21).

> "However, you may purchase male or female slaves from among the foreigners who live among you. You may also purchase the children of such resident foreigners, including those who have been born in your land. You may treat them as your property, passing them on to your children as a permanent inheritance. You may treat your slaves like this, but the people of Israel, your relatives, must never be treated this way"
>
> (Leviticus 25:44-46).

> "If a man sells his daughter as a servant, she is not to go free as male servants do"
>
> (Exodus 21:7).

> "Slaves, in reverent fear of God submit yourselves to your masters, not only to those who are good and considerate but also to those who are harsh"
>
> (1 Peter 2:18).

However, it is not so clear whether this is a valid criticism. When most of us think of slavery, what first comes to mind is the horrible abuse that African American people were subjected to in the American south for many years. Many other countries have also practiced slavery for quite a long time. According to current statistics, over fifty percent of people living in slavery live in just six countries: India, China, Pakistan, Bangladesh, Uzbekistan, and North Korea. It is certainly not an exaggeration to assert that the practice of race-based chattel slavery is one of the most despicable institutions ever to plague human civilization. However, it may be the case that slavery, as practiced in the Bible, is unlike the horrendous modern slavery phenomenon that most people conceptualize. Here are some Bible verses that support this perspective:

"There will always be poor people in the land. Therefore, I command you to be openhanded toward your fellow Israelites who are poor and needy in your land. If any of your people—Hebrew men or women—sell themselves to you and serve you six years, in the seventh year, you must let them go free. And when you release them, do not send them away empty-handed. Supply them liberally from your flock, your threshing floor, and your winepress. Give to them as the Lord your God has blessed you" (Deuteronomy 15:11-14).

> "Masters, provide your slaves with what is right and fair because you know that you also have a master in heaven" (Colossians 4:1).

> "If your brother with you becomes so poor that he sells himself to you, you are not to make him serve like a bond slave. Instead, he is to serve with you like a hired servant or a traveler who lives with you until the year of jubilee. Then he and his children with him may leave to return to his family and his ancestor's inheritance. Since they're my

servants whom I've brought out of the land of Egypt, they are not to be sold as slaves" (Leviticus 25:39-42).

"You are not to rule over them with harshness. You are to fear your God"

(Leviticus 25:43).

"And masters, treat your slaves in the same way. Do not threaten them, since you know that he who is both their Master and yours is in heaven, and there is no favoritism with him"

(Ephesians 6:9).

Another objection to the Bible involves its alleged moral inconsistency. Some scholars have contended that the Bible contains both good and evil teachings. Some of the immoral teachings cited are the command to kill adulterers, homosexuals, and people who work on the Sabbath. Another accusation is that the Bible permits ethnic cleansing (Exodus 34:11-14; Leviticus 26:7-9), genocide (Numbers 21:2-3, 33-35), and other forms of mass murder. Some have charged that the Bible endorses harsh attitudes toward children, the mentally handicapped, animals, the environment, people with unusual sexual habits, and older women. Even the New Testament has come under criticism since Jesus stated his objective was to cause family members to turn against each other so that they may love him more than their close relatives. There have been various other objections to the Bible, and I have tried to deal with the major ones.

CHAPTER 4

The Random Cruelty of Life: Murderous Dictators

History is replete with examples of unspeakable cruelty. Man's inhumanity to man has been on stark display since the beginning of human civilization. There has always been armed conflict somewhere in which people kill other people in the pursuit of power and control. Historians have estimated that over one hundred million people were murdered by their own government in the 20th century.

Perhaps the most prolific mass murderer in history is Chairman Mao Zedong of the People's Republic of China. As the head of the Communist Party of China, Chairman Mao launched an economic and social campaign known as the Great Leap Forward, which lasted from 1958 to 1962. This program aimed to transform China from a primarily agricultural economy into a socialist economy through rapid industrialization and collectivization. However, the program caused an enormous misallocation of resources leading to a dramatic reduction in food output and millions of deaths by starvation in the Great Chinese Famine.[4] One of this program's features was the introduction of mandatory agricultural collectivization in which the government prohibited private farming. Farmers who engaged in it could be subjected to social pressure and even persecution. Historians have stated that the Great Leap Forward resulted in the death of tens of millions of people. Chinese historian Yu Xiguang conducted thorough research and found the death toll may have been as high as fifty-six million people. According to historian Frank Dikötter, the basis of the Great Leap Forward was coercion, terror, and systematic violence, which resulted in one of the deadliest mass murders in human history.

As if the overwhelming hardship produced by the Great Leap Forward was not enough for the Chinese people to endure, in 1966, Chairman Mao initiated a sociopolitical movement known as the Cultural Revolution—formally known as the Great Proletarian Cultural Revolution. The revolution's stated objective was to preserve and solidify the Chinese Communist system by eradicating any vestiges of capitalism and other cancerous elements from Chinese society, thereby reinvigorating Maoism as the preeminent political ideology. According to many historians, the Cultural Revolution officially started in May 1966 when a document known as the May 16 Notification was issued by the Chinese Communist Party's Central Committee under Chairman Mao's direction. Partly in an attempt to restore his tarnished image after the monumental failure of the Great Leap Forward and to vanquish his political rivals, Mao gave a dire warning in this document that the CCP was being infiltrated by counter-revolutionary forces whose clandestine goal was to establish a "dictatorship of the bourgeoisie." He was confident that the movement he had launched would establish China as the glorious model for socialism worldwide and that he would be recognized as its principal architect.

In the weeks that followed, the CCP's official newspaper encouraged citizens, especially the youth, to instigate a concerted offensive to permanently dismantle the "four olds"—old ideas, old customs, old habits, and old culture. In response, Chinese students mobilized, forming para-military groups called Red Guards throughout the country. These groups engaged in wanton destruction of churches, shrines, libraries, shops, and private homes in a full-scale effort to eradicate ancient traditions. Moreover, party officials, teachers, and intellectuals were physically attacked and publicly humiliated; some were even murdered or driven to suicide. Mao's Defense Minister, Lin Biao, compiled the "Little Red Book" of Mao's quotations, and millions of copies were distributed to the public. However, the Red Guards began to degenerate into rival factions causing the country to plummet into a state of civil war. By the latter part of 1968, Mao came to the grim realization that the revolution had escalated out of control. In an attempt to subdue the raging violence, he ordered that millions of urban youth be relocated to the countryside to work with the peasant farmers as a form of re-education. The Peoples' Liberation Army attempted to restore order by any means, resulting in a massive increase in bloodshed and death. It was only with Chairman Mao's death in September 1976 that the Cultural Revolution finally came to an end. Estimates of the final death toll fluctuate wildly, from 500 thousand to as many as 20 million, along with a devastating impact on the Chinese economy. Mao's grandiose vision for a socialist utopia had disintegrated into a tragic failure for millions of people whose lives were ruined.[5]

One of the most brutal dictators of modern times was Communist leader Joseph Stalin. He served as leader of the Soviet Union from the mid-1920s until 1953 with the title General Secretary of the Communist Party of the Soviet Union. Stalin assumed leadership over the country following the death of Vladimir Lenin, the founder of the Soviet Union. Lenin served as the head of government of Soviet Russia from 1917 until his death in 1924. Stalin had thousands of people imprisoned and executed during his reign of terror. Anyone he regarded as a potential rival could be in grave danger, even close associates and members of his own family. His cruelty and disregard for human life were pathological, perhaps stemming from his severe paranoia. To eliminate alleged enemies of the state, Stalin created the "Great Purge," in which the government incarcerated over a million citizens and executed at least seven hundred thousand between 1934 and 1937. Realizing that Russia lagged considerably behind other countries in terms of industrial progress, Stalin devised and implemented three Five-Year Plans between 1928 and 1938 with the assistance of Gosplan, the Soviet State Planning Committee. The purpose of these plans was to promote economic development over limited periods utilizing quotas. The first two focused on developing heavy industry and the collectivization of farming at the expense of consumer goods production. Unfortunately, agricultural collectivization resulted in horrendous famines, particularly in Ukraine, where millions of people perished from starvation, disease, and bitterly cold weather. With the rapid ascent of Germany as a potential military rival, the third Five-Year Plan placed its primary emphasis on developing armaments.[6]

After WWII, Stalin was at the pinnacle of his career. Despite the psychopathic cruelty he had demonstrated throughout his years in power, the Russian people practically deified him as the epitome of indomitable leadership and patriotism. His *Collected Works* was published in 1946, followed by his official biography one year later in which he was exalted for his achievements. However, after he died in 1953, he was denounced by his successor Nikita Khrushchev for committing terrible crimes against the Russian people. A quote attributed to Joseph Stalin: "One death is a tragedy; one million is a statistic."[7]

Of course, no discussion of murderous dictators would be complete without mentioning Nazi leader Adolf Hitler, a genuinely deranged individual. Hitler became Chancellor of Germany in 1933 and was later proclaimed absolute Fuhrer in 1934. He is primarily responsible for starting World War II in Europe due to Poland's invasion in September 1939. Hitler was born in Austria and moved to Germany in 1913. German authorities imprisoned him in 1923 for attempting to seize power in a failed political coup, and it was there that he wrote his famous political manifesto, *Mein Kampf*. After his prison release in 1924, Hitler gained considerable popular support through his promotion of Pan-Germanism, anti-Semitism, and anti-Communism. He was a compelling public speaker who often condemned international capitalism and communism as part of a Jewish conspiracy. By July of 1932, the Nazi Party had become one of the largest political parties in Germany. President Paul von Hindenburg was persuaded by other German leaders to appoint Hitler as Chancellor in January 1933. After his rise to power, Hitler sought to establish a New Order whose purpose would be to counter what he perceived as the terrible hardships imposed on Germany after World War I. His government eliminated various restrictions and annexed territories in which millions of ethnic Germans lived.

It also directed a massive strengthening of the German military and, after the invasion of Poland in 1939, Britain and France declared war on Germany. Hitler ordered an invasion of the Soviet Union in June 1941 despite an agreement with Joseph Stalin not to do so. However, this campaign ultimately turned out to be disastrous. His failure to defeat the Soviets and the United States' entry into the war after the Japanese attack on Pearl Harbor forced the Nazi regime into a defensive position in which it sustained a series of humiliating defeats. In the last days of the war, Hitler married his longtime partner, Eva Braun, and on April 30, 1945, they committed suicide to avoid being captured by the Soviet Red Army. However, speculation persists to this day that Hitler may have escaped from his bunker and re-settled in Argentina.

It is widely known that Adolf Hitler harbored an intense hatred of the Jewish people, and the reasons for this have been the subject of extensive discussion. After his rise to power in 1933, he took steps to end Germany's democratic system by persuading his cabinet to allow the suspension of individual freedoms of press, speech, and assembly. The creation of security forces such as the Gestapo, the Storm Troopers, and the SS resulted in the arrest and murder of opposing political parties, including communists, socialists, and liberals. With the Enabling Act's passage in March 1933, the government essentially bestowed him with dictatorial powers. It was also at this time that the systematic harassment and persecution of Jews began. Jews living in Germany constituted less than one percent of the total population. Yet, the Nazi regime excluded them from various professions and sent many of them to concentration camps along with gypsies, homosexuals, disabled people, and other "undesirables" where the Nazis brutally murdered them as part of Hitler's

"Final Solution." Historians estimate that the Nazis executed approximately 5.5 million Jews in Germany and other countries.[8]

On April 17, 1975, a communist guerrilla army known as the Khmer Rouge, under the command of a Marxist revolutionary named Pol Pot, marched into Phnom Penh, Cambodia's capital city, and took control of the government. After a bitter civil war that lasted five years, and with support from North Vietnam and the Viet Cong, Pol Pot's soldiers, mainly consisting of teenage peasants, succeeded in conquering the Kingdom of Cambodia's government forces. Although the Cambodian people did not realize it at the time, they were about to be subjected to a nightmarish scenario of torture and genocide by one of the most bloodthirsty regimes of the 20th century.

Pol Pot proclaimed 1975 to be Year Zero after seizing power, marking the beginning of the country's purification. An ardent admirer of Mao Zedong, Pol Pot emulated the Chinese dictator with his version of the Cultural Revolution except to an even more extreme degree. One might think of it as a Cultural Revolution on steroids. His regime abolished all traces of Western culture, capitalism, urban life, and other foreign influences of any kind to give rise to a severe form of peasant Communism. The government forced the media to cease operations. It also expelled all foreigners, prohibited using money, shut down businesses, banned religion and education, eliminated health care, and revoked parental authority. The cities were forcibly evacuated, with two million Phnom Penh residents ordered at gunpoint to relocate to the countryside to engage in farming. In essence, Cambodia became isolated from the rest of the world.

The sheer depravity of the Khmer Rouge nearly defies description. From 1975 until 1979, approximately two million men, women, and children, which constituted about one-quarter of the total population, died of malnutrition or were tortured and killed in detention centers. Many of them were stabbed or bludgeoned to death to save ammunition, which was considered valuable. In particular, the regime targeted doctors, lawyers, teachers, intellectuals, former government officials, ex-soldiers, Buddhist monks, and anyone else who was considered representative of the old society. It also singled out ethnic minorities, including Chinese, Vietnamese, and Cham Muslims, for persecution. The Khmer Rouge cast the bones of all of these innocent victims into mass graves known as killing fields throughout Cambodia.[9]

On December 25, 1978, the Vietnamese military mounted a full-scale invasion of Cambodia to end the Khmer Rouge border attacks. On January 7, 1979, they succeeded in seizing control of the government in Phnom Penh, at which point Pol Pot was deposed. He sought refuge with the remnants of the Khmer Rouge in a remote jungle on the border with Thailand. Over the next seventeen years, he waged a guerrilla war against a succession of Cambodian governments with his depleted army. As a result of various internal power struggles during the 1990s, Pol Pot was forced to relinquish control and was placed under house arrest by his erstwhile comrades. Having been in poor health after suffering a stroke in 1995, he died in his sleep of an apparent heart attack on April 15, 1998, before facing an international tribunal to answer for his detestable crimes against humanity.

The continent of Africa has been subjected to more than its fair share of ruthless despots throughout history. One of the most brutal of these tyrants was Idi Amin Dada Oumee, who served as the President of Uganda from 1971 until 1979. His eight years of military dictatorship was characterized by widespread ethnic persecution, human rights violations, political corruption, and gross economic mismanagement. Popularly referred to as the "Butcher of Uganda," human rights organizations such as Amnesty International estimate that his highly repressive regime was responsible for as many as 500 thousand killings. Having received only an elementary education as a youth, Amin joined the King's African Rifles (KAR) in 1946. KAR was a regiment of the British colonial army. Amin quickly rose through the ranks, attaining Effendi's title, the highest possible position for a black African soldier within the KAR. An imposing physical specimen at 6 feet, 4 inches tall, and weighing two hundred forty pounds, Amin held Uganda's light heavyweight boxing championship from 1951 until 1960(One shudders to imagine how big the heavyweight champion of Uganda was at that time).

After more than seventy years under British colonial rule, Uganda achieved its independence on October 9, 1962, under the leadership of Milton Obote, a political activist and head of the Uganda People's Congress. He became Uganda's first Prime Minister on April 25, 1962. Amin, a close colleague of Obote's before his ascension to the office of Prime Minister, was promoted to Commander of the Army in 1965. By 1970, he was commander of all the armed forces of Uganda. However, a severe strain in their relationship developed in 1971 when Obote began to question Amin's loyalty due to possible misappropriation of military funds and Amin's suspected involvement in two failed assassination attempts on Obote's life. Amin became aware that Obote intended to have him placed under arrest. While Obote was attending a Commonwealth summit meeting in

Singapore, Amin and his troops took the offensive and staged a military coup. Obote found refuge in neighboring Tanzania, where he excoriated Amin as "the greatest brute an African mother has ever brought to life."

Initially, Uganda's people enthusiastically welcomed Amin with open arms, expecting that he would bring about positive change in the country. They viewed him not only as an influential military leader but as a charismatic man of the people. However, they were soon tragically disabused of this mistaken notion. Unknown to the general public, Amin was establishing death squads whose original responsibility was the extermination of soldiers he suspected of being loyal to Obote, resulting in the ruthless murder of as many as six thousand men. Amin's death squads, with outlandishly misleading names such as the Public Safety Unit and the State Research Bureau, also murdered farmers, students, clerks, and shopkeepers to confiscate their money and property. Moreover, his regime targeted members of various ethnic groups and religious leaders, journalists, artists, judges, lawyers, and intellectuals, all of whom they killed for ethnic, political, and financial reasons.

By the late 1970s, the international community became increasingly appalled by Amin's sadistic and eccentric behavior. As a clear indication of his megalomania, in 1977, he gave himself the ludicrous title of "His Excellency President for Life, Field Marshall Al Hadji Doctor Idi Amin, VC, DSO, MC, Lord of All the Beasts of the Earth and Fishes of the Sea, and Conqueror of the British Empire in Africa in General and Uganda in Particular" (No, I'm not kidding). He also fathered as many as fifty-four children with at least five wives, which proves that he did spend some time at home! In January 1979, as a result of ongoing military conflict with neighboring Tanzania, the Tanzania People's Defense Force, along with some Ugandan exiles, launched an invasion of Uganda. They captured Kampala, the capital city, on April 11, 1979, when Amin was forced to escape by helicopter. He first found refuge under Muammar Gaddafi in Libya, where he remained until 1980. He was then given sanctuary in Saudi Arabia by the Saudi royal family, who supported him financially in exchange for his promise never to become involved in politics. Amin died on August 16, 2003, of kidney failure without ever having expressed the slightest bit of remorse for his barbaric regime.[10]

Most people are familiar with Cuba's former communist leader, Fidel Castro, the longest-serving non-royal head of state since 1900. While a law student at the University of Havana, he became enamored with leftist anti-imperialist politics. He later became involved in revolts against right-wing governments in the Dominican Republic and Columbia. In 1959, Castro led a guerrilla movement that resulted in the overthrow of President Fulgencio Batista, after which he assumed full military and political power as Cuba's Prime Minister. The United States completely opposed Castro's Marxist-Leninist government and made some unsuccessful efforts to remove him from power using assassination, economic blockade, and counter-revolution. Castro aligned his government with the Soviet Union and allowed the Soviets to deploy nuclear weapons in Cuba in response to these threats. His action sparked the Cuban Missile Crisis, one of the tensest periods in the entire Cold War.

As absolute ruler of Cuba, Castro converted the island-nation into a socialist state under Communist Party rule, which had never been seen before in the Western Hemisphere. His policies included centralized economic planning, state control of the press, and the total suppression of political dissent. Under Castro's iron fist, thousands of Cubans were thrown into prison, where they suffered under horrendous conditions. His regime subjected many more to systematic harassment and intimidation and denied fundamental political rights to entire generations. As stated by José Miguel Vivanco, America's director at Human Rights Watch: "Castro's draconian rule and the harsh punishments he meted out to dissidents kept his repressive system rooted firmly in place for decades."[11]

The Middle East has been a hotbed of violence and bloodshed for centuries. Many brutal dictators have emerged from this region throughout history. In recent times, one of the most egregious of these dictators was Iraqi leader Saddam Hussein. Hussein served as President of Iraq from July 1979 until April 2003. Before gaining full presidential power in 1979, he served as vice president under General Ahmed Hassan al-Bakr. Since the general had been in poor health for some years, Hussein effectively controlled Iraq's government long before forcing al-Bakr's resignation and taking control. He maintained power during a turbulent period that saw both the Iran-Iraq War and the Gulf War with the United States. Hussein was widely criticized for his regime's brutality, earning him the dubious title "Butcher of Baghdad." His security forces murdered approximately two hundred fifty-thousand Iraqis through various purges and genocides. Moreover, his invasions of Iran and Kuwait resulted in the death of hundreds of thousands of innocent people.

In 2003, the United States led a coalition of forces in a successful military operation to depose Hussein. His Ba'ath party was effectively disbanded, and free elections were then held. The United States military captured Hussein in December 2003, and an Interim Iraqi Government put him on trial. In November 2006, an Iraqi court convicted him of crimes against humanity for his murderous activities as President of Iraq. He was executed by hanging on December 30, 2006.[12]

Another notorious Middle Eastern leader of the late 20th century is Muammar al-Qaddafi of Libya. On September 1, 1969, he assumed power as the leader of a group of young Libyan military officers who successfully deposed King Idris I in a bloodless coup d'état. At the age of twenty-seven, he was designated chairman of the Revolutionary Command Council, Libya's ruling class, and Commander in Chief of the armed forces. Shortly after taking control, Qaddafi ordered the closure of American and British military bases in Libya. He also demanded a higher percentage of revenue from foreign oil companies operating in Libya. Furthermore, he instituted laws that criminalized any form of political dissent to safeguard his regime from potential coup attempts.[13]

Qaddafi's style of leadership was not merely repressive; rather, it bordered on absurd. He was often accompanied by a group of female bodyguards known as the Amazonian Guard, thought of himself as the royal leader of Africa, had an elaborate tent constructed which he used when traveling abroad, and dressed in outlandish outfits resembling costumes. His bizarre behavior, which served as somewhat of a distraction from his cruelty, earned him the nickname "the mad dog of the Middle East."[14] He was also rich beyond the dreams of avarice, having amassed a mind-boggling fortune in oil revenue estimated to be as high as $200 billion. His family, friends, and business associates became extremely wealthy while most Libyan citizens languished in abject poverty. Moreover, his regime was linked to some horrific terrorist attacks, the most notable being the 1988 bombing of Pan Am flight 103 over Lockerbie, Scotland, in which all 259 passengers perished along with eleven civilians on the ground.

In 2003, he accepted responsibility for the bombing, and compensation was paid to the victims' families, many of whom were American. However, he denied ever having given the order for the attack.

After more than forty years as an absolute ruler of Libya, Qaddafi's empire began to unravel in 2011 with surprising rapidity. The Arab Spring, which started in Tunisia with a local vendor's martyrdom, quickly spread to other Arab countries such as Egypt, Yemen, Syria, Bahrain, and Libya. Shortly after the Tunisian uprising, citizens drove Egyptian President Hosni Mubarak from office, which encouraged protesters in other Arab countries to intensify their anti-government activities. Qaddafi attempted to brutally suppress the demonstrations with the use of police and foreign mercenaries; however, violence continued to escalate as more Libyans became resolute in their determination to remove him from office. By the end of February 2011, they had seized power in much of Libya and formed a governing body known as the National Transitional Council, which was supported by most of the international community. Shortly after that, a NATO coalition undertook a series of airstrikes supporting rebel forces, which proved to be the decisive blow. Qaddafi, who had gone into hiding, was assassinated near Sirte, Libya, on October 20, 2011.[15]

The nation of North Korea has been prominently featured in the news for some years, especially since the election of Donald Trump as President of the United States. North Korea's blatant nuclear ambitions have been a source of deep concern to the Trump administration. The ruler of this highly secretive dictatorship, known as the "Hermit Kingdom,"[16] is Kim Jong-un, the son of former leader Kim Jong-il and grandson of Kim Il-sung, the first leader of North Korea who ruled since its establishment in 1948 until he died in 1994. While it is true that Kim Jong-un has instituted some economic and agricultural reforms, he has continued, unabated, the dreadful human rights violations and vicious suppression of political opposition, which was characteristic of the two previous regimes. Such violations include arbitrary arrest, torture, rape, starvation, imprisonment in brutal labor camps, and public execution. He has also ordered the murder of family members, including his uncle and half-brother.[17] President Trump has unequivocally condemned North Korea's reckless pursuit of nuclear weapons, referring to Kim Jong-un as "rocket man." In turn, Kim has labeled President Trump a deranged old man. Needless to say, such vitriolic rhetoric has not been well received by either of these leaders. Nevertheless, they have had a few reasonably cordial meetings in which President Trump has suggested the possibility of a "new future" for North Korea.[18] Perhaps this is a reason for optimism, although experience has demonstrated that North Korean dictators are not the most trustworthy people in the world.

Of course, many other brutal dictators throughout history inflicted unimaginable suffering on their people. Some glaring examples include Benito Mussolini in Italy, Francisco Franco in Spain, Hideki Tojo in Japan, and Robert Mugabe in Zimbabwe, just to mention a few on this extensive and tragic list. I find it highly unlikely that a Divine Being could have permitted so many utterly wicked people to rise to such lofty positions of power.

CHAPTER 5

The Random Cruelty of Life: 20th Century Natural Disasters

Another disturbing example of the random cruelty of life is the phenomenon of natural disasters worldwide that have beset humankind since the dawn of civilization. A natural disaster is a sudden, catastrophic event that results in widespread devastation, including enormous loss of life, severe property damage, and substantial financial loss. Natural disasters have occurred worldwide for centuries, and the United States has been no stranger to these cataclysmic events.

The deadliest natural disaster in US history is the Great Galveston Hurricane of 1900. This storm slammed into the city of Galveston, Texas, on September 8, 1900, with sustained winds of over one hundred thirty-five miles per hour and a fifteen-foot storm surge. The storm caused six thousand to twelve thousand fatalities on Galveston Island and the mainland. Meteorologists retroactively classified it as a Category 4 hurricane on the Saffir-Simpson Hurricane Wind Scale[19]. Meteorologist Robert Simpson and structural engineer Herbert Saffir developed this scale in response to Hurricane Camille. This Category 5 storm struck the Mississippi Gulf Coast on August 17, 1969, with sustained winds of one hundred ninety miles per hour and a twenty-five-foot storm surge. Camille is the most powerful hurricane to strike the US mainland since the government began keeping records in 1851.[20]

Even looking back over the past twenty years, a dauntingly large number of natural disasters have plagued the United States. One of the most memorable is Hurricane Katrina, which made its initial landfall on August 25, 2005, at Hallandale Beach and Aventura in Florida. After weakening slightly to a tropical storm, Katrina entered the Gulf of Mexico's warm waters, where it began to intensify, reaching Category 5 status. However, the storm weakened to Category 3 strength shortly before making its second landfall on August 29, when its right front quadrant crashed into Gulfport, Mississippi, producing immense damage. Katrina caused tremendous destruction along most of the Gulf Coast since the storm was approximately four hundred miles across. The city of New Orleans witnessed some of the worst damage since its levee system was unable to withstand the force of Katrina. As a result, as many as twenty-three breaches in the drainage canal and navigational canal levees and floodwalls occurred. A final estimate of the number of fatalities was at least 1,836 — with many of them in New Orleans. The total property damage was approximately one hundred twenty-five billion dollars, the highest in US history to that point in time.[21]

In 2017, the United States and Puerto Rico were struck by three major hurricanes in rapid succession: Harvey, Irma, and Maria. Hurricane Harvey was the eighth named storm and the first major hurricane of the 2017 Atlantic hurricane season, a very active one. Harvey originated in the Lesser Antilles' east as a tropical wave and reached low storm status on August 17. It weakened somewhat due to moderate wind shear until it entered the Bay of Campeche on August 23. At that time, it began to intensify, attaining hurricane status later that day. Harvey made its initial landfall at San José Island, Texas, as a Category 4 storm, followed by another landfall at Holiday Beach. It then rapidly weakened and was downgraded to a tropical storm as it remained relatively stationary over the Texas coast. Several locations in the Houston metropolitan area received at least thirty inches of rain, with a maximum of sixty-four and a half inches in Nederland, Texas. This rainfall amount is the heaviest ever recorded in the US during a tropical storm, easily surpassing Hawaii's 1950 record of fifty-two inches. The total rainfall that fell on Houston is the heaviest in that city since Tropical Storm Allison inundated it with torrential rain in 2001 (Allison's name was retired although the storm never reached hurricane strength).[22] In terms of financial loss, Harvey rivals Hurricane Katrina as the costliest hurricane ever recorded, causing approximately one hundred twenty-five billion dollars in property damage, primarily from catastrophic flooding in the Houston metropolitan area and the Southeast Texas coast.[23]

Following on Harvey's heels was Hurricane Irma, the ninth named storm, the fourth hurricane, the second major hurricane, and the first Category 5 hurricane of the 2017 season. Irma developed from a tropical wave near the Cape Verde Islands, an archipelago of ten volcanic islands in the central Atlantic Ocean. A relatively large number of hurricanes have begun life in this part of the Atlantic Ocean. Irma rapidly intensified and reached Category 3 status on the Saffir-Simpson Scale on August 31. Over the next few days, the storm alternated between a Category 2 and a Category 3, owing to a series of eyewall replacement cycles. On September 4, Irma resumed intensification, reaching Category 5 strength the following day with sustained winds of one hundred eighty-five miles per hour, making it the most intense storm worldwide for the 2017 season. Irma caused unprecedented damage in Barbuda, Saint Barthelemy, Saint Martin, Anguilla, and the Virgin Islands as a Category 5 hurricane. The storm made landfall on September 10 as a Category 4 hurricane on Cudjoe Key, Florida, making a second landfall on Marco Island. It rapidly weakened and dissipated on September 13 over the state of Missouri. Irma caused extensive flooding in Florida and is the costliest storm in its history, with over fifty billion dollars in total property damage.

Shortly after that, in September 2017, Hurricane Maria devastated Dominica, the US Virgin Islands, and especially Puerto Rico with Category 4 to Category 5 ferocity. Maria was the thirteenth named storm, the fourth major hurricane, the second Category 5 hurricane, and the deadliest storm of the highly active 2017 Atlantic hurricane season. It developed from a tropical wave into a low-level storm east of the Lesser Antilles on September 16. Due to favorable environmental factors, the storm quickly intensified before slamming into the island of Dominica as a Category 5 hurricane. After weakening while traveling overland, Maria struck Puerto Rico as a powerful Category 4 storm, causing massive damage and loss of life. The storm later traveled east-northeast over the open Atlantic, becoming extratropical and dissolving by October 2nd. Nearly one year later, the official tally indicated 2,975 fatalities in Puerto Rico, sixty-five in Dominica, five in the Dominican Republic, four in Guadeloupe, four in the contiguous United States, three in the United States Virgin Islands, and three in Haiti, bringing the death toll to 3,059. Total financial losses from Hurricane Maria were estimated at more than $91.6 billion, primarily in Puerto Rico, thus ranking it as the third costliest hurricane ever recorded.[24]

The 2018 Atlantic hurricane season was the third consecutive season with higher than average hurricane activity. Many forecasters had predicted moderate activity due to relatively cold sea surface temperatures in the tropical Atlantic and an El Nino weather pattern's expected development. However, this pattern did not materialize in time to suppress weather activity that surpassed what most forecasters had expected. During the 2018 season, there were fifteen named storms, eight hurricanes, and two major hurricanes, resulting in a total financial loss of over fifty billion dollars in damages.

The first severe storm of the 2018 season was Hurricane Florence, which made landfall in the United States just south of Wrightsville Beach, North Carolina. Although the storm had attained Category 4 strength at various times after initially forming near the Cape Verde islands, it weakened to a Category 1 hurricane by the time it reached the US coastline. Florence traveled inland very slowly while drenching coastal areas with tremendous rainfall. As a result, widespread flooding occurred along a lengthy stretch of the North Carolina coast, inundating the cities of Fayetteville, Smithfield, Lumberton, Durham, and Chapel Hill. On September 17, the storm weakened to a post-tropical cyclone over West Virginia and was absorbed into another storm two days later. Florence caused at least fifty-four deaths, with financial losses in the United States exceeding twenty-four billion dollars.

The second, and by far the most severe storm to strike the United States in the 2018 season was Hurricane Michael. Michael was the first Category 5 hurricane to hit the contiguous United States since Hurricane Andrew in August 1992. It was also the fourth most intense Atlantic hurricane on record to make landfall in the contiguous United States. It is surpassed only by the 1935 Labor

Day Hurricane, which struck the lower Florida Keys, Hurricane Camille, which ravaged the Mississippi Gulf Coast in August 1969, and Hurricane Andrew, which struck South Florida in August 1992. Michael was the thirteenth named storm, seventh hurricane, and the second major hurricane of the season. It developed from a low-pressure area in the southwestern Caribbean Sea on October 1 and became a tropical depression on October 7. The storm rapidly intensified as it traveled over the Gulf of Mexico's warm waters, and as it approached the Florida Panhandle on October 10, it reached Category 5 status. Michael caused catastrophic damage in the Florida Panhandle, especially in Mexico Beach and Panama City. It then headed in a northeastward direction toward the Chesapeake Bay, transitioning into an extratropical cyclone over southern Virginia before dissipating on October 16. Hurricane Michael directly caused at least seventy-four fatalities in the United States and Central America, along with over twenty-five billion dollars in total damage.[25]

Hurricanes were not the only natural disaster that struck the United States and other countries in recent years. The 2018 global wildfire season was disastrous with massive, seemingly out-of-control wildfires in France, Germany, Greece, Sweden, Finland, Norway, Latvia, Canada, Spain, and Great Britain. In July 2018, there was even an extremely unusual wildfire that broke out north of the Arctic Circle on the Russia-Finland border near the Barents Sea.[26] A great deal of attention has been focused on recent wildfires in the western United States, where approximately 8.8 million acres of forest land were incinerated during the 2018 season compared to about ten million in 2017. These disastrous fires hit the state of California particularly hard. According to the California Department of Forestry and Fire Protection and the National Interagency Fire Center, the

2018 wildfire season was the deadliest and most destructive ever recorded in California, with a total of 8,527 fires consuming an area of 1,893,913 acres—the highest amount of acreage ever destroyed in a single season. In terms of monetary loss, these fires resulted in over $3.5 billion in damages. The Mendocino Complex Fire, which occurred in Mendocino, Lake, Colusa, and Glenn Counties in northern California, was a large combination of two wildfires, the River Fire and the Ranch Fire. They were first reported on July 27, 2018, and destroyed over 459,000 acres before being completely contained on September 18. The Mendocino Complex Fire was the most massive complex fire in the state's history to that point in time[27]. During July and August, other large wildfires also developed in the northern part of the state, including the horrific Carr Fire. This wildfire took place in Shasta and Trinity Counties, burning 229,651 acres before being contained on August 30, 2018. The outbreak of these highly destructive and costly wildfires caused state officials to declare a national disaster on August 4, 2018, approved by President Trump.[28]

In November 2018, the devastating Camp Fire in Butte County, California, replaced the Mendocino Complex Fire as the deadliest and most destructive wildfire in California history. It consumed 153,336 acres and destroyed approximately eighteen thousand buildings before being contained on November 25, 2018, after burning for seventeen days. The total damage in monetary terms was about $16.5 billion. As a result of this wildfire, the town of Paradise, California, was virtually wiped off the face of the earth in a matter of eight hours. Officials thought that the fire started due to damage that occurred in a power line near the small community of Pulga, although this has not been clearly established. Pacific Gas and Electric, the largest electric utility company in the country, based on the number of customers, was subsequently inundated with over a thousand law-suits, demanding compensation for damages. These lawsuits rep-resented thousands of individuals, companies, cities, and counties deeply affected by the wildfires. In response to this legal onslaught, the utility filed for bankruptcy protection on January 29, 2019.[29]

Around the same time that the Camp Fire was overwhelm-ing northern California, the Woolsey Fire was wreaking havoc in Southern California, mainly in Los Angeles and Ventura Counties. It burned 96,949 acres, destroyed 1,643 structures, and caused the evacuation of over two hundred ninety-five thousand residents. The fire is believed to have started on November 8 in Woolsey Canyon on the Santa Susana Field Laboratory property, a complex of industrial research and development facilities owned by the Boeing Company.[30] Driven by the powerful Santa Ana winds, the fire traveled in a south-erly direction for the entire first day. It barreled through the steep canyons, destroying historical movie and TV sets, small ranches, and the homes of some well-known celebrities. Some homes in the wealthy, coastal community of Malibu were either completely oblit-erated or damaged to some degree. The fire was finally completely contained on November 21, with a total cost from property damage between four billion and six billion dollars.[31]

In 2019, severe wildfires occurred in the Amazon rainforest, Australia, Canada, Indonesia, the Mediterranean, and Siberia. One of the chief reasons cited for these fires is climate change resulting in drier vegetation and a more extended wildfire season. Other factors include a decrease in rainfall for that year, aging energy infrastruc-ture, rapid deforestation due to farming and logging, and a higher number of people living near heavily wooded areas. Scientists and environmentalists have urged governments worldwide to focus greater attention on the threat of wildfires so that countries do not reach a point where ecosystems become unmanageable.[32]

However, except for Alaska, the United States witnessed a dramatic decline in wildfire destruction compared to the previous two years, reaching its lowest level since 2004. Alaska typically experiences the most wildfires, although they tend to occur in remote areas with little threat to local communities. The National Interagency Fire Center, which tracks significant wildfires in the US, cautions that 2019 was an exception and should not be viewed as a reliable predictor of future wildfire activity.[33]

Other countries have also been devastated by natural disasters since 2000. On March 11, 2011, at 2:46 PM local time, a magnitude-9.0 undersea earthquake occurred approximately forty-five miles off the northeast coast of Japan's Honshu island. It was the most powerful earthquake ever recorded in Japan and the fourth most powerful in history. It caused the planet to shift on its axis, according to a study conducted by the US Geological Service. This event, referred to as "The Great East Japan Earthquake,"[34] generated a titanic tsunami that inundated over 200 square miles of coastal land. Some of the waves were estimated to be as high as an astounding 130 feet.

According to a report by the National Police Agency of Japan, over one million buildings were either demolished or damaged to some degree, and extensive structural damage occurred in northeastern Japan to roads and railways. The tsunami inflicted severe damage to nuclear power plants, especially at three reactors in the Fukushima Daiichi Nuclear Power Plant complex, which experienced meltdowns and the evacuation of hundreds of thousands of residents in the immediate area. The combined total of confirmed deaths and missing was well over 20,000. According to an estimate by the World Bank, the financial cost was as high as $235 billion, making it the costliest natural disaster in world history.[35]

On the afternoon of May 12, 2008, a magnitude-7.9 to 8.0 earthquake, known as the Sichuan Earthquake of 2008 or the Great Wenchuan Earthquake, occurred in the mountainous central region of Sichuan province in southwestern China. The quake resulted from a collision of the Indian-Australian and Eurasian plates along the 155-mile long Longmenshan Fault, which stretches southwest to northeast along the eastern side of the Longmen Mountains and separates the Plateau of Tibet from the flat Sichuan Basin. The earthquake inflicted massive damage in the Sichuan province, completely demolishing nearly eighty percent of the structures and causing about 90,000 fatalities, making it the deadliest earthquake in China since the Tangshan Earthquake of 1976. It also left an estimated 4.8 million to 11 million homeless residents, the highest homeless count from a natural disaster in recorded history. Another tragic consequence of the earthquake: tens of thousands of schoolchildren perished in school buildings that collapsed because they had been constructed with substandard building methods.[36] The initial quake was followed by numerous aftershocks for several months, resulting in additional casualties and property damage. Within one week after the disaster, China formally requested aid from the international community, which quickly responded along with donations from people and organizations throughout mainland China. On November 6, 2008, the Chinese government announced that it would spend approximately $146.5 billion over three years to rebuild areas severely impacted by the earthquake.[37]

On May 2, 2008, Cyclone Nargis, a powerful tropical storm, made landfall in Myanmar (formerly Burma) in the northern Indian Ocean. It destroyed the Irrawaddy Delta Region, which is the lowest expanse of land in Myanmar, in only two days. The storm developed from a low-pressure system in the Bay of Bengal during the last week of April and began to travel in a northeastward direction. By May 2, it attained peak intensity with sustained winds of 135 miles per hour, equivalent to a Category 4 hurricane on the Saffir-Simpson Hurricane Wind Scale. The storm made landfall in southwest Myanmar near the town of Wagon in the Ayeyarwady Division. Rather than traveling directly inland as many tropical storm systems tend to do, Nargis remained along the Irrawaddy Delta coast, which inhibited the rapid weakening associated with tropical storms as they move over land. Authorities estimated that the storm seriously impacted over 2 million people, with about 1 million losing their homes due to structural damage. Although we may never know the cyclone's actual death toll, the figure given is around 138,000, with total property damage close to $13 billion, making Nargis the costliest storm to have ever occurred in the North Indian Ocean basin.[38]

On the morning of December 26, 2004, an undersea megathrust earthquake registering a magnitude of 9.1 to 9.3 occurred approximately 100 miles off the western coast of northern Sumatra at a depth of about 19 miles. It was estimated to have had the energy of 23,000 Hiroshima-strength atomic bombs. The earthquake took place along a tectonic subduction zone where the India Plate slid beneath the Burma microplate, part of the larger Sunda Plate. As a result of this underwater seismic activity, a series of massive tsunami waves, measuring up to 100 feet, were generated. The waves traveled across the Indian Ocean at a jet plane's speed, killing an estimated

230,000 people in fourteen countries. Most of the fatalities occurred in Indonesia, where over 200,000 perished, especially in northern Sumatra's Aceh province. Numerous deaths also occurred in Sri Lanka, India, the Maldives, and Thailand, all of which sustained enormous economic damage. The tsunami claimed its final victims 5,000 miles away on the coast of South Africa. The total financial cost resulting from property damage was at least $15 billion. The 2004 Indian Ocean Tsunami is the deadliest in recorded history.[39]

The nation of North Korea suffered through a devastating famine, along with a general economic crisis from roughly 1994 to 1998. Estimates of the death toll range from 240,000 to 3,500,000 out of a total population of approximately 25 million. There were several contributing factors to the North Korean famine, also known as the Arduous March or the March of Suffering. A misguided policy of isolationism and self-sufficiency by North Korea's socialist government was unquestionably a key factor. The dissolution of the Soviet Union, which had been providing considerable financial aid, along with food supplies and cheap fuel, also played a significant role. The North Korean government was in complete control of food distribution, and it favored members of the military and residents of urban areas while leaving less privileged citizens such as farmers, the elderly, and children to fend for themselves. A warm El Nino weather pattern, starting in 1995, caused pervasive flooding, which destroyed at least 15 percent of the nation's farmland, greatly exacerbating the food shortage. Eventually, the North Korean government requested assistance from the international community, which was initially reluctant to help. However, global food assistance gradually moderated the famine, although some food supplies were stolen and redistributed among the country's elite classes. According to the

United Nations, many North Koreans still lack adequate nutrition and primary healthcare and sanitation access. A UN report in 2019 indicated that over 40 percent of the population is malnourished.[40]

Pandemics are generally not classified as natural disasters. A pandemic is an epidemic that has spread to several countries or continents, affecting many people. If we ranked pandemics as natural disasters, then the deadliest natural disaster in recorded history would be the Spanish influenza of 1918. With a death toll from 40 million to 100 million people, it's referred to as "the mother of all pandemics."[41] In all likelihood, the total number of fatalities resulting from this influenza exceeds the combined number of deaths from WWI, WWII, the Korean War, and the Vietnam War, a truly staggering figure. The term "Spanish Flu" is a misnomer since this dreadful plague probably did not originate in Spain. Wartime censors simply downplayed initial reports of illness and deaths in Germany, Great Britain, France, and the United States so as not to dampen morale. However, the Spanish media freely informed the public of its existence. There are varying theories regarding this pandemic's origin. Some identify an overcrowded hospital in northern France; others maintain that it first appeared at a military base in Haskell County, Kansas, while others claim that it probably started in China.[42]

Historians have described the Spanish influenza as "the greatest medical holocaust in history,"[43] reaching nearly every country in the world with catastrophic results. Almost 17 million people in India alone succumbed to the flu, which constituted about 5 percent of the population. Many other countries also experienced high mortality rates. The typical mortality rate from a flu epidemic is about 0.01 percent, whereas this worldwide pandemic brought about the demise of about 20 percent of those infected. One unusual feature of the Spanish flu was that it killed many young adults between the ages of 20 and 40, whereas most flu outbreaks tend to be far more lethal to infants, the elderly, and those with compromised immune systems. It also acted with astonishing speed, with many of those infected dying within twelve hours from the time symptoms first manifested themselves. The Spanish flu's first wave was relatively benign, with most reasonably healthy people recovering rather quickly. However, in the second wave, which began around August 1918, the flu virus mutated into a far more sinister form, with the most fatalities occurring in October 1918. By the end of 1918, reported cases diminished dramatically, probably because the virus had mutated to a considerably less lethal strain. As to the possibility of a worldwide influenza pandemic happening again, the scientific community's consensus is that we are better prepared to deal with such a phenomenon thanks to significant advances in medical technology.[44]

CHAPTER 6

The Random Cruelty of Life: The Deadliest Natural Disasters

It might appear that the 20th century has witnessed some of the deadliest natural disasters in history, but this is not at all the case. On the contrary, the total death toll from natural disasters in the 20th century pales compared to the total number of fatalities sustained worldwide throughout recorded history. Excluding ancient natural disasters for which reliable data is not available, it is possible to ascertain the ten deadliest natural disasters with reasonable accuracy based on the historical record—a veritable top-ten hit parade of incomprehensible tragedies. Six of these appalling events occurred in China, two in India, one in Haiti, and one in East Pakistan, which is now Bangladesh. The reader should take note that this list is not universally agreed upon by authorities on the subject.

The tenth deadliest natural disaster in recorded history is the 1920 Haiyuan earthquake, which occurred on December 16, in Haiyuan County, Ningxia Province, in the Republic of China. This earthquake, which reportedly measured 7.8 on the Richter scale, was followed by an amazingly long period of aftershocks that lasted for three years. It caused rivers to change course and sent massive landslides hurtling down from mountaintops. Severe destruction spanned across seven Chinese provinces, encompassing some twenty-five thousand square miles, including ten heavily populated areas. The death toll was approximately 273,400, including people killed by the original earthquake and its numerous aftershocks and those who perished in the severe winter that followed the quake. The large-scale havoc was caused primarily by poor soil conditions throughout the region.[45]

The ninth deadliest natural disaster in recorded history is the 1976 Tangshan earthquake. It measured between 7.8 and 8.2 on the Richter scale and struck the region around Tangshan, Hebei, in the northeastern part of the People's Republic of China on July 28, 1976. At 3:42 that morning, Tangshan's busy industrial city, with a population of about one million residents, was all but annihilated in a matter of minutes. More than eighty percent of the city's bridges collapsed or were rendered unusable, all public services failed, and most highway and railway bridges collapsed or were heavily damaged. A severe aftershock occurred later that day, measuring 7.1 on the Richter scale, in Luanxian, about forty-three miles to the northeast. This aftershock resulted in additional damage and casualties and hindered attempts to rescue people already trapped beneath the rubble. Many strong aftershocks were felt in the region for several months following the original earthquake. The total number of fatalities is estimated to range from two hundred forty-two thousand up to six hundred fifty-five thousand, but the actual death toll may never be known with complete certainty. The Chinese government's official account states that 242,769 people were killed, and 169,851 were severely injured. However, based on the population's density and the extreme nature of the damage, the actual death toll may have been as much as three times greater than the official government report stated. The earthquake took place along a previously unknown fault, which is now known as the Tangshan Fault. Eventually, Tangshan was rebuilt with much stronger earthquake precautions, and its current population is nearly two million people.[46]

The eighth deadliest natural disaster in recorded history is the 1737 Calcutta cyclone. Also known as the Hooghly River Cyclone, this storm made landfall inside the Ganges River Delta just south of Calcutta. It generated a storm surge of thirty to forty feet—comparable to the 1839 Coringa Cyclone. Observers initially thought that an earthquake caused the cyclone, but they did not verify that theory. Reportedly, fifteen inches of rain fell on the region within six hours. Overall, the storm destroyed roughly twenty thousand vessels, ranging from ocean-worthy ships to small canoes. The final death toll, including ship's crews and the local population, has been reported from three hundred thousand to three hundred fifty thousand.[47]

The seventh deadliest natural disaster in recorded history is the 1839 India cyclone, which struck the bustling port city of Coringa in Andhra Pradesh province on the Bay of Bengal on November 25. Andhra Pradesh is one of India's twenty-nine states and is situated in the country's southeast, covering 61,855 miles. Coringa is a small village located close to the mouth of the Godavari River on the southeastern coast. Although there are no reliable measurements of the maximum wind speed, the storm surge was as high as a phenomenal forty feet. The total number of fatalities resulting from this storm was roughly three hundred thousand. Coringa was never fully rebuilt after this calamitous cyclone, and today remains a simple, coastal village. Henry Piddington, an official with the British East India Company, coined the term "cyclone" after studying the damage caused by this storm, which he described as a "swirling circle."[48]

The sixth deadliest natural disaster in recorded history is the 2010 Haiti earthquake, which occurred on January 12, 2010, about sixteen miles west of Port-au-Prince, Haiti's capital city. This earthquake measured 7.0 on the Richter scale and was followed by a series of at least fifty-two aftershocks, measuring 4.5 or higher. The estimate of total fatalities is somewhat controversial, ranging from one hundred thousand to three hundred sixteen thousand, which is the upper limit of the Haitian government's range. The capital city of Port-au-Prince, along with Jacmel and other cities in the region, experienced significant property damage, including the Presidential Palace and the National Assembly building. Many countries, along with organizations such as the International Committee of the Red Cross and Doctors Without Borders, provided humanitarian aid during the ensuing crisis. The island of Hispaniola, which Haiti and the Dominican Republic share, is a seismically active area and has a history of damaging earthquakes that scientists have documented over the years. The island has also been struck rather frequently by tropical cyclones, which have caused extensive flooding and sweeping damage. Most recently, Tropical Storm Fay and Hurricanes Gustav, Hanna, and Ike struck the island, all in the summer of 2008, resulting in almost eight hundred deaths.[49]

The fifth deadliest natural disaster in recorded history is the 1970 Bhola cyclone, which occurred on November 13, 1970, in East Pakistan (now Bangladesh) and India's West Bengal state. It was the deadliest cyclone ever recorded. At least five hundred thousand people perished in the storm, many of them due to the overpowering storm surge which deluged a large portion of the low-lying islands of the Ganges Delta. The cyclone developed from the remnants of a tropical storm dissipating in the Pacific Ocean, resulting in a tropical depression in the Bay of Bengal on November 8. It then traveled in a northward direction toward East Pakistan, intensifying along the way. On November 11, the cyclone attained its maximum intensity with sustained winds of approximately one hundred fifteen miles per hour. It made landfall the following afternoon, causing massive destruction to East Pakistan, the coastal islands, and the heavily populated delta region. Regrettably, the Bhola cyclone is not the only tropical cyclone that has resulted in many fatalities in Bangladesh. Based on a report from the Bangladesh Meteorological Department, there have been ten tropical cyclones since 1876 with death tolls of five thousand or more. Four of these cyclones were responsible for one hundred thousand or more fatalities.

Another consequence of the Bhola cyclone was widespread political unrest in East Pakistan. Many residents of the region viewed the response by the Pakistan government to be wholly inadequate. After the hurricane struck only three weeks before the country's first democratic elections, the Awami League of East Pakistan based its campaign on the complete indifference of the ruling Pakistani elite to this tragedy. As a result, they managed to achieve a landslide victory in their home province, which served as justification for their leader, Sheikh Mujib, to assume power. However, the Pakistan government had no intention of allowing this to occur, which left no choice for the Awami League but to declare their independence. After a vicious attack by the Pakistan military, followed by nine months of guerrilla warfare and India's intervention, the nation of Bangladesh was created.[50]

The fourth deadliest natural disaster and the deadliest earthquake in recorded history is the 1556 Shaanxi earthquake, which struck the province of Shaanxi in Northwestern China on the morning of January 23, 1556. It leveled a five hundred twenty-mile wide area around its epicenter, and in some counties, as much as sixty percent of the population perished. Many inhabitants lived in artificial caves called yaodongs, which they carved out of high cliffs in the Loess Plateau. This plateau covered the majority of the Shanxi, Shaanxi, and Gansu provinces, where the earthquake was most destructive. The Loess Plateau consisted mostly of highly erosion-prone soil, quite vulnerable to wind and water forces. The earthquake caused many of these caves to collapse, thereby contributing heavily to the massive fatalities. The death toll ranged from eight hundred twenty thousand to eight hundred thirty thousand people. The total financial loss resulting from property damage is incalculable since an entire region of Northwestern China was eradicated in less than one day.[51]

It would appear that the Big Man Upstairs has it in for the Chinese people. We can only speculate as to what horrible iniquities they have perpetrated on humanity over the centuries. Setting aside fairy tale explanations such as this, China has the geological misfortune of being caught between the Indian and Pacific tectonic plates. For this and other technical reasons, China has been the object of unusually active, seismic activity throughout history. In an average year, eighteen earthquakes of magnitude 5.0 or greater on the Richter scale strike China. Six out of thirteen of the deadliest earthquakes to assault our planet have occurred in China.

The third deadliest natural disaster in recorded history is the 1887 Yellow River flood, which started on or around September 28,

1887. The Yellow River is about three thousand miles long, and its origin is well above sea level in the northern mountain province of Qinghai, in the northwest region of China. For centuries, farmers living close to the river constructed dikes to contain the continually rising waters caused by silt accumulation on the riverbed. In late September 1887, this rising riverbed, exacerbated by a long summer of intense rainfall, overwhelmed its dikes resulting in extensive flooding of the surrounding farmland. The flooding swept away over three hundred villages and eleven major cities as it relentlessly surged forward over more than fifty thousand square miles. Virulent diseases such as typhus and dysentery inevitably followed, thereby seriously magnifying the death toll. The total number of inhabitants who succumbed to the flooding, disease, and famine ranged from nine hundred thousand to two million. The Yellow River has been referred to as "The Cradle of Chinese Civilization" and "China's Sorrow." The latter description pays tribute to the millions who have tragically lost their lives over the centuries. The Yellow River has flooded a recorded 1,593 times over four millennia, with dire consequences for the surrounding population.[52]

The second deadliest natural disaster in recorded history is the 1931 China flood event, a series of catastrophic floods in the Republic of China. China suffered through a prolonged drought from 1928 to 1930, followed by an exceptionally severe winter. In the spring of 1931, large deposits of ice and snow, which had accumulated in central China's mountainous areas, melted and flowed downstream into the Yangtze River during a period of unusually heavy spring rain. The result was a deluge that forced residents of low-lying areas to abandon their homes. Further complicating the situation, high cyclonic activity occurred during the summer. This unfortunate combination of meteorological circumstances resulted in an inundation that extended over an area of approximately 111,847 miles (a size roughly equivalent to the total area of New York, New Jersey, and Connecticut combined). In late August, a high-water mark in Wuhan, the capital of Central China's Hubei province, indicated the water level to be roughly fifty-three feet above normal. The total death toll from flooding, famine, and disease was 3.7 to four million people. The Yangtze River, which is the longest river in Asia and the third-longest worldwide, has been both a blessing and a curse to the Chinese people. It has been highly beneficial regarding transportation, fishing, and farming. However, it has also flooded numerous times over the centuries, resulting in unimaginable property damage and loss of life.[53]

The deadliest natural disaster in recorded history is the 1876 drought and famine in China, which struck the five northern provinces of Shandong, Zhili, Shanxi, Henan, and Shaanxi. A severe drought started in north China in 1875, which led to alarming crop failures. It persisted into the early summer months of 1879. As a result, many residents of the region migrated to other parts of China. By the time the rainfall amounts returned to relative normalcy, an estimated nine million to thirteen million residents of the affected area's total population of approximately one hundred eight million had succumbed to famine and famine-related diseases. An international relief network was established to request donations, much of which came from England and foreign businesses operating in China. The Shandong Famine Relief Committee was created in March 1877, involving business people, foreign diplomats, and Protestant and Roman Catholic missionaries. Based on an evaluation of historical documents, the 1876-1878 North China drought was identified as the most severe drought to have occurred over the past three hundred years preceding this tragic event.[54]

Having researched these calamities which have tormented humanity over the centuries, it is difficult for me to believe that a loving, heavenly father figure whom we refer to as God could allow such prodigious devastation and loss of life over such a protracted period. Is human life so cheap to this celestial entity that He can permit untold millions of people to die horrible deaths with little or no warning? Christians like to say that God's ways are unsearchable, but I would suggest that God's ways are psychotic. In my opinion, God requires intensive psychotherapy in order to cure Him of His homicidal tendencies.

CHAPTER 7

The Random Cruelty of Life: Mass Shootings

Another horrifying example of the random cruelty of life is the phenomenon of mass shootings around the world. The only mass shooting that I can recall from the 1960s and 70s occurred on August 1, 1966. On this day, a 25-year-old former Marine sharp-shooter named Charles Whitman ascended to the observation deck at the top of the central building tower at the University of Texas at Austin with seven weapons and an enormous supply of ammunition. For approximately ninety minutes, he fired upon people on the ground with devastating accuracy, killing fourteen and wounding at least thirty others. He was then shot and killed by some courageous Austin police officers who had reached the observation deck. Whitman had fatally stabbed his wife and mother the previous night. An autopsy revealed that he had a tumor in a part of the brain known as the amygdala, which is crucial for rational judgment and behavioral control. He also had kept a journal in which he described violent fantasies that continually besieged him.[55] At the time, this event was unprecedented and sent shock waves through the entire nation.

52

However, for the past twenty years, these horrific shootings have been occurring with alarming frequency.

On August 3, 2019, a 21-year-old man named Patrick Crusius entered a Walmart Supercenter near the Cielo Vista Mall in El Paso, Texas. He opened fire on shoppers with a semi-automatic version of an AK-47 rifle. After killing twenty-three people and wounding twenty-three others, he drove to a nearby intersection and surrendered to an El Paso motorcycle officer, identifying himself as the perpetrator. The FBI investigated the shooting as a hate crime and an act of domestic terrorism. Crusius reportedly posted an online manifesto in which he condemned Texas's alleged Hispanic invasion and expressed support for the shooter who murdered fifty-one people and injured forty-nine others at mosques in Christchurch, New Zealand earlier that year.[56]

Less than fourteen hours after the El Paso tragedy, on August 4, 2019, a 24-year-old man named Connor Betts fatally shot nine people while wounding twenty-seven others outside of a bar in the Oregon Historic District of Dayton, Ohio. Within one-minute, local law enforcement officers, who were already at the scene of the massacre, shot and killed Betts. Authorities learned that he had been suspended from Bellbrook High School for compiling a list of students he wanted to murder and rape, which resulted in a police investigation. His high school girlfriend stated that he reported having visual and auditory hallucinations and was fearful of developing schizophrenia. He also had performed with a band that was fixated on dark, sinister themes involving necrophilia and other forms of sexual violence.[57]

On the afternoon of May 31, 2019, a 40-year-old city employee named Dewayne Craddock entered Building 2 of the Virginia Beach

Municipal Center armed with two .45-caliber handguns. He fatally
shot twelve people and wounded five others, three of them critically.
Afterward, he exchanged gunfire with police while taking refuge in
an office on the second floor. Officers breached the door of the office
where they found him to be grievously wounded. He died on the way
to the hospital.[58] Craddock served as an engineer in the city's public
utility department, and his job performance was considered satis-
factory. A few hours before the attack, he tendered his resignation in
an email to city management, citing personal reasons. He reportedly
had been involved in altercations with fellow employees in the days
before his deadly rampage. However, he had no previous criminal
record other than minor traffic violations. A few neighbors in his
apartment building described him as a loner with very few friends.[59]

On March 15, 2019, a 28-year-old Australian man named
Brenton Tarrant entered the Al Noor Mosque in a suburb of
Christchurch, New Zealand, and began firing indiscriminately at
worshippers. He brought two semi-automatic rifles and two shot-
guns to the mosque. A witness stated that the gunman played military music from a portable speaker during his rampage. Tarrant
then returned to his vehicle to retrieve another weapon, after which
he returned to the mosque to continue the slaughter. After spend-
ing less than ten minutes at the Al Noor Mosque, he drove to the
Linwood Islamic Center, about three miles east, where he continued
his murderous frenzy. Police apprehended Tarrant within thirty minutes after the first emergency call to local authorities by ramming his
vehicle against a curb and arresting him at gunpoint. They charged
him with fifty-one murders, forty attempted murders, and engaging
in a terrorist act. He initially pleaded not guilty to all charges with a
trial set for May 2020, but changed his plea to guilty on all counts on

March 25, 2020, and was sentenced to life in prison without the possibility of parole.[6061] Within a month following the massacre, the New Zealand Parliament under Prime Minister Jacinda Ardern voted 119 to 1 to ban military-style semi-automatic weapons and the components used to build them. Authorities determined that Tarrant had connections to far-right extremist organizations and began planning his brutal attack about two years in advance. As in the El Paso killer case, he authored a manifesto in which he expressed strong anti-immigrant sentiments and advocated forcibly removing all non-European immigrants from Europe. He also professed admiration for the Norwegian terrorist and mass murderer Anders Breivik and cited him as a source of inspiration.

On November 7, 2018, at approximately 11:20 PM, a 28-year-old United States Marine Corps veteran named Ian David Long approached the Borderline Bar and Grill's entrance in Thousand Oaks, California. He carried a .45-caliber Glock 21 semi-automatic handgun equipped with a laser sight. He also had seven illegal, high-capacity magazines, each containing thirty rounds. First, he fatally shot a security guard outside of the building and then charged into the nightclub, firing randomly at patrons and employees. Shortly after the club made an emergency call, police officers and a SWAT team entered the building to pursue the gunman, who they found deceased in the kitchen from a self-inflicted gunshot wound. He had killed twelve people and injured about twelve others in the chaotic scene.[62] Ian Long served in Afghanistan from November 2010 to June 2011, earning several awards from the Marine Corps, including a Combat Action Ribbon and a Marine Corps Good Conduct Medal. He had no criminal record. However, Long later exhibited behavior that may have been symptomatic of post-traumatic stress disorder.

In April 2018, deputies were called to his home in Newbury Park, California, regarding a disturbance in which he acted in a somewhat angry, irrational manner. Mental health specialists evaluated him to determine if they should commit him under California state law 5150, which allows for the temporary, involuntary psychiatric confinement of individuals who appear to present a danger to themselves or others due to a mental disorder. However, they concluded that such action was not justified.[63]

On the morning of October 27, 2018, a 46-year-old white nationalist named Robert Bowers entered the Tree of Life Synagogue in Pittsburgh, Pennsylvania, armed with a Colt AR-15 semi-automatic rifle and three Glock .357 semi-automatic handguns. He began firing on worshippers in various parts of the building before being confronted by police and SWAT team members, with whom he exchanged gunfire before retreating to a room on the building's third floor. After a brief period and being wounded, Bowers surrendered. While receiving medical treatment, he reportedly told a SWAT officer that he wished for all Jews to die for committing genocide against his people. In the course of his rampage, Bowers killed eleven and wounded at least six others. The US Department of Justice charged him with twenty-nine federal crimes for which federal prosecutors sought the death penalty. Bowers had been actively involved in social media and was quite sympathetic to neo-Nazis, white supremacists, and other far-right organizations. On a website known as Gab, he stated that Jews are Satan's children and supported the white genocide conspiracy theory. He was also critical of President Trump, who Bowers alleged was being controlled by Jews who surrounded him.[64]

On October 17, 2018, a mass shooting and bombing attack occurred at the Kerch Polytechnic College in Kerch, Crimea, a former

Soviet Union territory. An 18-year-old student named Vladislav Roslyakov, a senior at the college, entered the grounds at approximately 11:45 a.m. and began shooting randomly at classmates and faculty with a Hatsan Escort Aimguard 12-gauge, pump-action shotgun. According to witnesses, his shooting spree went on for at least fifteen minutes as he calmly walked the hallways firing his weapon at anyone he saw, as well as shooting at computer monitors, locked doors, and fire extinguishers. He also detonated a powerful, improvised explosive device rigged with shrapnel, which blew out some windows, causing further serious injuries. The brutal carnage came to an end when the gunman committed suicide in the school library. The final tally of his onslaught was twenty fatalities and seventy injuries, some of them critical.[65]

Roslyakov's parents divorced when he was about ten years old after his father sustained a debilitating head injury and became belligerent toward family members and other relatives. As a student, Roslyakov's grades were mediocre, and he had very few friends. He enrolled at the Kerch Polytechnic College in 2015 intending to study to become an electrician. During his time in college, he developed a fascination with explosives and weapons and completed training at a local shooting range to legally obtain a gun and ammunition. He also became involved in several online communities devoted to serial killers.[66] As an admirer of Eric Harris and Dylan Klebold, Roslyakov's hideous crime bore some eerie similarities to the Columbine High School massacre on April 20, 1999. He dressed in dark pants and a white t-shirt during his rampage—as did Eric Harris; he detonated a powerful explosive in the school cafeteria—as the Columbine duo attempted to do; he committed suicide in the library—as Harris and Klebold did after exchanging gunfire with the police. There have been numerous copycat crimes spawned by the 1999 Columbine massacre, which has led to the coining of the term "Columbine Effect."

On the morning of May 18, 2018, a 17-year-old student named Dimitrios Pagourtzis entered Santa Fe High School in the metropolitan Houston, Texas, area armed with a short-barreled, 12-gauge Remington Model 870 pump-action shotgun and a Rossi .38-caliber, snub-nosed revolver. He had stolen the weapons, concealed under a dark trench coat, from his father, who owned them legally. Pagourtzis made his way to the school's art complex, which consisted of four rooms connected by interior hallways. According to one witness, Pagourtzis casually strolled into one of the classrooms while singing the song "Another One Bites the Dust" by the rock band Queen and proceeded to fire at students. In a panic, they barricaded themselves in a storage closet, at which point Pagourtzis shot through the door with his shotgun, killing at least one student. After leaving the classroom, he was confronted by police officers stationed at the school, one of whom Pagourtzis critically injured, although the officer survived the attack. Pagourtzis was then engaged by another school officer and a Texas State Trooper who attempted to convince him to surrender peacefully. However, Pagourtzis fired more rounds while screaming at the officers and only surrendered after being wounded. His horrifying assault, which lasted for nearly twenty-five minutes, resulted in ten fatalities—eight students and two teachers—as well as thirteen injuries. This attack is the third deadliest high school shooting in United States history, surpassed only by the Columbine High School massacre of 1999 and the Marjory Stoneman Douglas High School shooting in Parkland, Florida, which occurred just three months before this incident.[67]

Pagourtzis was taken into custody and held without bail at the Galveston County Jail charged with multiple persons' capital murder and aggravated assault of a public servant. He had provided minimal warning as to the monstrous crime he was about to commit. An honor roll student who also played on the junior varsity football team, some of his teachers described Pagourtzis as a quiet, non-threatening young man. However, other witnesses reported that he had been the victim of bullying by several students and some of his coaches, although school authorities disputed the accusations of bullying by faculty members. A few weeks before the shooting, he posted a photo of a shirt with the words "Born to Kill" on his Facebook page. He stated to authorities that he had intended to commit suicide after the shooting but could not end his own life. Since he was seventeen at the time of the incident, Pagourtzis was ruled ineligible for the death penalty, with the maximum allowable sentence being forty years to life in prison. On November 4, 2019, three independent psychiatric experts determined that he was mentally unfit to stand trial. Officials transferred him to the North Texas State Hospital in Vernon, Texas, a highly restricted inpatient mental health facility whose purpose is to treat people with mental illnesses after local mental health authorities have screened them.[68]

On February 14, 2018, a 19-year-old former student at the Marjory Stoneman Douglas High School in Parkland, Florida named Nikolas Cruz entered the building and began firing on his former classmates and staff members with an AR-15 rifle. Cruz's violent rampage resulted in the death of seventeen people and the wounding of seventeen others. He escaped from the area by blending in with other students but was apprehended about an hour later in the nearby town of Coral Springs. He was placed in the Broward County

Jail and separated from the other inmates due to his high-profile status. His fatal attack is the deadliest high school massacre in American history. Cruz was adopted at birth, and both of his adoptive parents died before the mass shooting. He displayed behavioral problems since middle-school and was transferred six times in the following three years. According to state investigators, Cruz suffered from depression, autism, and attention deficit hyperactivity disorder(ADHD). However, they concluded that he did not appear to be at a high risk of harming himself or those around him.[69]

On November 5, 2017, 26-year-old Devin Patrick Kelley of New Braunfels, Texas, fatally shot twenty-six people and wounded twenty others at the First Baptist Church in Sutherland Springs, Texas (about thirty miles east of San Antonio). Kelley arrived at the church shortly after eleven o'clock in a white Ford Explorer and parked close to the door. He dressed in black tactical gear, a ballistic vest, a black facemask with a white skull, and armed with a Ruger AR-556 semi-automatic rifle. After fatally shooting two people outside of the church, Kelley began firing at the building itself. He then entered the church through a side door and, screaming an obscenity, proceeded to fire at worshippers in the pews. Local authorities stated that he fired as many as seven hundred rounds during a frenetic shooting spree that went on for almost eleven minutes. He was then confronted by a heroic resident named Stephen Willeford, a former NRA instructor armed with an AR-15 rifle. They briefly exchanged gunfire, after which Kelley fled in his Explorer. Soon after that, he was found dead in his vehicle with three bullet wounds, including a self-inflicted head wound.[70] Authorities later determined that Kelley had a violent past, including a vicious assault on his wife, resulting in a one-year sentence in a military prison and a bad-conduct

discharge from the Air Force in 2014. His shocking attack on innocent churchgoers is the deadliest mass shooting in Texas history.[71]

On the night of October 1, 2017, 64-year-old Stephen Paddock
began firing into a crowd of concertgoers at the Route 91 Harvest
Music Festival on the Las Vegas Strip from his hotel room on the
32nd floor of the Mandalay Bay Hotel and Casino. Paddock killed
sixty people and wounded over four hundred others before committing suicide through a self-inflicted gunshot wound. This incident is
the deadliest mass shooting by a lone gunman in American history.
Paddock served as an agent for the Internal Revenue Service in the
late seventies and early eighties. He also worked as an accountant
and successful real estate investor with personal property and apartment buildings in California and Texas. According to IRS records,
Paddock made over five million dollars in 2015 from the sale of an
apartment complex purchased in 2004. He was also a devoted gam-
bler whose favorite game was video poker. In the months before the
massacre, Paddock was reportedly drinking heavily and taking the
prescription anti-anxiety drug valium, which can be a dangerous
combination. Based on the information provided by the Bureau
of Alcohol, Tobacco, Firearms, and Explosives, starting in October
2016, he began purchasing numerous firearms, mainly rifles, as well
as firearm-related accessories. After his meticulously planned attack
and suicide, law enforcement officials discovered an enormous arsenal of weapons inside the hotel rooms that he had occupied. They
sent his remains to Stanford University for extensive analysis, and
no abnormalities were found within his brain.[72]

On the evening of July 7, 2016, residents held a peaceful protest in downtown Dallas, Texas. Approximately eight hundred people attended, along with one hundred police officers assigned to

monitor the event. The Next Generation Action Network organized the demonstration in response to the shooting death by police officers of two African American men: Alton Sterling in Baton Rouge, Louisiana, and Philando Castile in Falcon Heights, Minnesota, which had occurred just days before the protest. At approximately 9:00 p.m., as the rally was concluding, a 25-year-old man named Micah Xavier Johnson parked his SUV next to El Centro College, occupying a city block in downtown Dallas. Johnson began shooting at police, and protesters gathered on Main Street just south of the college with a semi-automatic rifle. As a result of the initial gunfire, he killed three officers, wounded at least three others, and one civilian. Although it was difficult for them to determine where the shots were coming from, other officers returned fire. The gunman fired so rapidly that it seemed as if there might be multiple shooters, although they later determined that he acted alone. After fatally shooting a fourth officer, Johnson took refuge in building B of the college. Situated in a mezzanine facing Elm Street to the north, he shot out numerous windows. He began firing on officers on the ground, striking and killing another officer. Johnson then secured himself in an area filled with offices and the school's computer servers, which was relatively inaccessible to the police. Officers attempted to initiate negotiations with the gunman, who indicated that he would only communicate with black police officers. According to Dallas Police Chief David Brown, Johnson gave the impression of being delusional and derisive during the standoff, laughing, singing, and inquiring as to how many officers he had killed. At approximately 2:30 a.m., Chief Brown realized that negotiations were futile, and the shooter would have to be taken out by other means. He ordered the deployment of a bomb disposal remote control vehicle, which police equipped with about one pound of C-4 explosive. They maneuvered it to a point against a wall facing the gunman, at which time the explosive material was detonated, killing Johnson instantly. This was the first time in the history of US law enforcement that a robot was used to end the life of a suspect, in addition to being the deadliest single incident for US law enforcement since the September 11th attacks.[73]

Originally from Magee, Mississippi, Micah Xavier Johnson grew up in the quiet Dallas suburb of Mesquite, Texas. His childhood was relatively uneventful other than the divorce of his parents when he was four years old. After high school, Johnson served in the US Army Reserves from March 2009 to April 2015 and was deployed to Afghanistan from November 2013 to July 2014. During his time there, he was accused of sexual harassment by a female soldier who requested that a protective order be issued against him and suggested that he receive mental health counseling due to his aggressive behavior. However, he was honorably discharged in September 2014, although this may have been due to an administrative error. According to the documentation provided by the Veterans Health Administration, Johnson exhibited symptoms of post-traumatic stress disorder (PTSD) after his return from Afghanistan. Doctors gave him medication for anxiety, depression, hallucinations, and panic attacks. After the shooting, a search of his home resulted in the recovery of bomb-making materials, rifles, ammunition, and ballistic vests, along with a journal of combat tactics. He also received training at a private self-defense school that involved rapid shooting on the move to conceal his location and create the impression of multiple shooters. Johnson was an individual who gave every indication of preparing for a deadly attack.[74]

On the night of June 12, 2016, a 29-year-old security guard named Omar Mateen, also known as Omar Mir Seddique, shot and killed forty-nine people and wounded fifty-three others inside Pulse, a gay nightclub in Orlando, Florida. After a three-hour standoff, he was shot and killed by Orlando police officers. The FBI had investigated Mateen in 2013 and 2014 and placed him in the Terrorist Screening Database for possible connections to terrorist organizations. However, for some reason, they later removed him from the database.[75] He identified himself as an "Islamic Soldier" and pledged his allegiance to Abu al-Baghdadi, a militant jihadist leader. Mateen claimed that the shooting was in retaliation for an airstrike in Iraq that killed Abu Wahib, an ISIL commander. His ex-wife described him as an unstable individual with violent tendencies.[76] At the time, this shooting was the deadliest mass murder in the United States since the September 11 attacks in 2001, although it was surpassed by the Las Vegas massacre a little over one year later.

On the morning of December 2, 2015, a married couple, Syed Rizwan Farook and Tashfeen Malik, armed with semi-automatic pistols and rifles, fatally shot fourteen people and wounded twenty-two others at the Inland Regional Center in San Bernardino, California. Farook was a US citizen of Pakistani descent, and Malik was a Pakistani-born green cardholder. The San Bernardino Department of Public Health, which employed Farook as a health department worker, held a public health training exercise and Christmas party with approximately eighty employees in a rented banquet room at the time of the shooting. Afterward, the couple fled in a Ford Expedition. Four hours later, police located and pursued the vehicle in a suburban neighborhood about two miles from the massacre site. The couple engaged them in a violent shootout, which lasted for about five minutes, resulting in the two perpetrators' deaths and injuries to two officers.[77] The FBI conducted an investigation and described the couple as homegrown violent extremists who had been inspired by foreign terrorist organizations. However, they were not instructed by any such groups to carry out this heinous act and had no affiliation with any known terrorist cell or network.[78] Their vicious attack was the deadliest mass shooting in the US since the Sandy Hook Elementary School massacre in 2012 and the most lethal terrorist assault in the US since the September 11 tragedy.

On June 17, 2015, a 21-year-old white supremacist named Dylann Storm Roof fatally shot nine African American churchgoers, including the pastor, during an evening prayer service at the Emanuel African Episcopal Church in Charleston, South Carolina. Roof sat quietly in the back of the church for approximately one hour before drawing a Glock .45-caliber handgun and firing multiple times at parishioners while uttering some racially inflammatory statements. He later admitted to authorities that he was attempting to ignite a race war.

After the shooting, Roof fled the scene and was apprehended the following morning in Shelby, North Carolina, thanks to a tip from an observant motorist. He was returned to South Carolina to stand trial, where he was convicted in federal court of thirty-three charges, including hate crimes, for which he received a death sentence.[79] On March 31, 2017, he agreed to plead guilty in South Carolina state court to nine counts of murder, three counts of attempted murder, and possession of a firearm during the commission of a felony. For these crimes, he received nine consecutive sentences of life without the possibility of parole. On April 22, 2017, authorities transferred him from the Al Cannon Detention Center in North Charleston, South Carolina, to the Terre Haute Federal Prison in Indiana, a facility that incarcerates male inmates awaiting execution under federal law.

On December 14, 2012, 20-year-old Adam Lanza walked into the Sandy Hook Elementary School in Newtown, Connecticut. He fired on students and staff members using a Bushmaster XM15-E2S rifle and a Glock 20SF handgun. Lanza killed twenty children (all between six and seven years old) and six adult staff members before killing himself. He had previously shot and killed his mother at their Newtown home. While in fifth-grade, Lanza had written a book with a classmate detailing a litany of violent fantasies, including homicide and bank robbery.[80] He also spent an excessive amount of time playing violent video games and appeared to display an obsessive interest in firearms. After showing signs of extreme anxiety and difficulty with social interaction, he was diagnosed with Asperger's Syndrome in 2005. However, mental health professionals who had contact with him in high school did not report making any observations that could have predicted his future behavior.[81]

On July 20, 2012, 32-year-old James Holmes entered a Century 16 movie theater in Aurora, Colorado, during a midnight screening of *The Dark Knight Rises* and began firing at the audience. Holmes killed twelve people and injured seventy others before being apprehended by police. His attorney subsequently entered a plea of not guilty by reason of insanity, but the prosecution sought the death penalty. The jury found him to be guilty, and on August 7, 2015, they sentenced him to life in prison without the possibility of parole.[82] Before his trial, forensic psychiatrist Dr. William H. Reid spent months reviewing over 80,000 pages of documentation pertaining to the case and conducting nine personal interviews with Holmes. Dr. Reid testified that Holmes was mentally ill but legally sane, diagnosing him as having a schizotypal personality disorder characterized by constrained behavior and problems relating to other people.[83]

On July 22, 2011, 40-year-old Anders Breivik murdered seventy-seven people in a bomb attack in Oslo, Norway, and a mass shooting at a summer camp for children on Utoya, an island off the coast of Norway. In July 2012, he was convicted of mass murder, causing a fatal explosion, and terrorism. He is currently serving a twenty-one-year sentence in prison near Skien, Norway.[84] Shortly before the attacks, Breivik emailed a manifesto entitled *2083: A European Declaration of Independence. He* voiced his opposition to Islam and blamed feminism for what he described as a cultural suicide in Europe. Before his trial, two teams of court-appointed forensic psychiatrists examined him. The first team diagnosed him as suffering from paranoid schizophrenia. However, the second team stated that he was not psychotic but had a narcissistic personality disorder and antisocial personality disorder.[85]

On the morning of January 8, 2011, US Representative Gabrielle Giffords of Arizona was conducting a meeting with constituents in the parking lot of a Safeway supermarket in Casas Adobes, north of Tucson. The conference, called "Congress on Your Corner," started at 10 a.m. After approximately ten minutes, a 22-year-old man named Jared Lee Loughner emerged from the crowd of twenty to thirty people brandishing a Glock 19 semi-automatic pistol with a 33-round magazine. He shot Congresswoman Giffords in the head at point-blank range and then began firing at other people in attendance. While reloading his weapon, Loughner was tackled and subdued by a 74-year-old retired Army colonel who had also been shot, with help from other bystanders. Within minutes, police and paramedics arrived at the scene and took Loughner into custody. As a result of the attack, nineteen people were shot, with six fatalities. The deceased included Federal District Court Judge John Roll, a member of Gifford's staff named Gabe Zimmerman, and a nine-year-old girl named Christina-Taylor Green. Loughner was uncooperative with authorities, invoking his right to remain silent under the Fifth Amendment. In January 2012, a federal judge found him incompetent to stand trial based on two medical evaluations in which he was diagnosed with paranoid schizophrenia. However, after receiving antipsychotic medication while in jail, he was judged competent in August. In November 2012, he was sentenced to serve seven consecutive life terms plus 140 years in prison without the possibility of parole.[86] He is currently incarcerated at the Federal Medical Center in Rochester, Minnesota, a facility for male inmates who require specialized or long-term medical or mental health care.

Friends of Loughner reported that he seemed to undergo a radical personality transformation around eighteen years of age and was no longer the sweet, caring person they remembered. After a breakup with his high school girlfriend, he started to abuse alcohol and other drugs, including marijuana, cocaine, psychedelic mushrooms, and LSD. He was suspended from Pima Community College, which he attended from February to September of 2010, for bizarre, disruptive behavior that some of his teachers interpreted as a sign of incipient mental illness. In the months before the shooting, Loughner's parents became so concerned over the disturbing behavior that they disabled his car every night to prevent him from leaving the house. Clearly, he was a deeply troubled young man, but the warning signs of potentially violent behavior were not taken seriously enough by those around him to seek professional help.[87]

Gabrielle Giffords regained some of her physical and cognitive ability thanks to intensive therapy at the Memorial Hermann Medical Center in Houston, Texas, and a facility in Asheville, North Carolina. Upon her return to the House of Representatives' floor in August 2011, she was greeted with a standing ovation. She formally submitted her resignation from the House on January 25, 2012. Her husband, Mark E. Kelly, a US Navy Captain and NASA astronaut, published a memoir in 2011 entitled *Gabby: A Story of Courage and Hope,* in which he credited her with co-authorship. The couple also created a political action committee known as Americans for Responsible Solutions, whose stated purpose is to prevent access to guns by dangerous individuals, including criminals, terrorists, and people with a mental illness.

On November 5, 2009, Nidal Hasan, A 39-year-old US Army major and psychiatrist, fatally shot thirteen people and wounded more than thirty others at the Fort Hood military base near Killeen, Texas. Immediately afterward, Hasan was shot, which resulted in paralysis from his waist down. On July 30, 2011, he was charged with thirteen counts of premeditated murder and thirty-two counts of attempted murder under the Uniform Code of Military Justice. Military authorities sentenced him to death on August 28, 2013. Shortly after the mass shooting occurred, the media reported that a Joint Terrorism Task Force had been aware of multiple emails between Hasan and Imam Anwar al-Awlaki, a Yemen-based individual who the NSA had been monitoring as a potential security threat. Some coworkers stated that Hasan's behavior appeared to be increasingly radical in the years before the shooting. He is currently on death row at the United States Disciplinary Barracks at Fort

Leavenworth, Kansas. This tragic event is the deadliest mass shooting ever to take place on an American military base.[88]

The deadliest school shooting in US history occurred on April 16, 2007, at the Virginia Polytechnic Institute and State University in Blacksburg, Virginia. A 23-year-old undergraduate student and US resident named Seung-Hui Cho, originally from South Korea, shot forty-nine people on campus using two semi-automatic pistols. The result of his rampage was thirty-two deaths and seventeen injuries. When police entered the building in pursuit, Cho committed suicide through a self-inflicted gunshot wound to the head. Officials later determined that he had previously been diagnosed with a severe anxiety disorder and had undergone therapy during his middle and high school years. However, due to federal privacy laws, this information was not made available to the authorities at Virginia Tech.[89]

On October 2, 2006, 32-year-old Charles Carl Roberts IV entered the West Nickel Mines School, a one-room schoolhouse in the Old Order Amish community of Nickel Mines, Pennsylvania, and held ten young girls hostage. Shortly after that, he shot eight of them, killing five and wounding three others. As a state trooper approached a window of the schoolhouse, Roberts committed suicide. Before his death, he stated in a phone call to his wife that he had molested two young female relatives twenty years previously, a charge that was denied by both girls. Roberts left a suicide note to his wife and one to each of his three children; these notes also alluded to anger, which he bore against God. An autopsy did not reveal the presence of drugs nor any brain abnormalities.[90]

On March 21, 2005, 16-year-old Jeffrey Weise committed mass murder on the Red Lake Indian Reservation in Red Lake, Minnesota. Weise first shot and killed his grandfather, who was a tribal police officer, and the grandfather's girlfriend at their home. He then took the grandfather's police weapons and vest and drove his vehicle to Red Lake Senior High School, where Weise had been a student. He shot and killed seven people and wounded five others. Among the dead were an unarmed security guard, a teacher, and five students. After exchanging gunfire with the police, he retreated to a vacant classroom where he committed suicide with a shotgun. Weise had a troubled family life and had attempted suicide twice. His doctor treated him for depression with Prozac, and his dosage level was increased to 60mg per day merely a week before his shooting spree. He also reportedly was the victim of taunting and bullying by some classmates.[91]

On April 26, 2002, a mass shooting occurred at the Gutenberg-Gymnasium in the Thuringia State capital, Erfurt, Germany (a German Gymnasium is comparable to an American high school). On this day, 19-year-old former student Robert Steinhauser, who had previously been expelled, entered the building armed with a 9mm Glock pistol and a Mossberg 590 Mariner 12-gauge pump-action shotgun. He fatally shot sixteen people while wounding one other person. The victims included thirteen staff members, two students, and one police officer. According to some students, Steinhauser seemed to ignore them during his shooting spree and focused more on the teachers and school administrators. However, he inadvertently shot and killed two students through a locked door. He then turned one of the guns on himself and committed suicide. Concerning his motive for this brutal massacre, officials reported that Steinhauser was enraged with the school administrators over his expulsion.[92]

Of course, most of us remember the infamous shooting massacre and attempted bombing on April 20, 1999, at Columbine High School in Littleton, Colorado.[93] Two seniors, Eric Harris and Dylan Klebold shot and killed twelve students and one teacher using an arsenal of weapons. It included a Hi-Point 995 Carbine with thirteen 10-round magazines, a Savage Springfield 67H pump-action shotgun, a 9x19mm Intratec TEC-9 semi-automatic handgun, and a Stevens 311D double-barreled shotgun. Friends purchased these weapons at gun shows since Harris and Klebold were too young to buy guns legally. The duo also injured twenty-three people and planted several homemade bombs, the largest of which they placed in the cafeteria. The bombs failed to detonate; if they had, the carnage would have been much more extensive. The gunmen exchanged gunfire with police before committing suicide in the school library. They had planned the attack for at least one year and were hoping that it would rival or surpass the Oklahoma City bombing on April 19, 1995.[94]

In 1996, Eric Harris created a private website on America Online based on the popular video games *Doom* and *Doom II*. He also started a blog on the website that consisted primarily of jokes, thoughts about his family and friends, and school life. However, the blog also referred to some vandalism acts, such as setting off fireworks that he had committed with his friend Dylan Klebold and others. At the time, Harris worked at a fireworks stand where they gave him some fireworks. In the early months of 1997, his blog postings began to take on a more sinister tone, wherein he expressed his anger and resentment toward society in general. By the end of that year, the website provided detailed instructions in the assembly of explosive devices. Despite this disturbing development, the website received very little attention until March 1998 when he concluded a blog post by delineating some violent fantasies alluding to his intense desire to murder and injure as many people as possible, making a specific reference to a classmate. The parents of this young man became aware of the threat and, deeply concerned, contacted the Jefferson County Sheriff's office requesting an investigation. The investigating officer gained access to Harris's website, where he discovered a litany of aggressive threats directed against Columbine High School students and faculty members. The officer wrote a draft affidavit in which he requested a search warrant of the Harris household. Unfortunately, the testimony was not submitted to a judge, and no action was taken.[95]

Harris and Klebold were arrested on January 30, 1998, near Littleton, Colorado, after breaking into a van and stealing tools and computer equipment. They pled guilty to felony theft and were ordered to attend classes, including anger management, as part of a juvenile diversion program. Harris wrote a letter of apology to the van owner in which he seemed to be very apologetic and respectful. However, in his journal, he expressed indignation at being arrested and blamed the van owner for leaving his tools on the front seat. Klebold swore revenge for the arrest and specifically mentioned the mayhem they would create in the school cafeteria. Nearly a year before the massacre, Klebold wrote a message in Harris's 1998 yearbook in which he declared his strong desire to kill his enemies, including police officers. In their journals, they documented their arsenal and plan of attack in meticulous detail, including diagrams. They also produced some videos in which they discussed their terrifying plans and reasons for the impending slaughter. They made a final video less than one hour before the deadly assault, where they said goodbye and expressed their apologies to friends and families for the unspeakable act they were about to commit.[96]

The FBI conducted an exhaustive investigation of the shooting, resulting in thousands of pages of documentation. The report described Eric Harris as a clinical psychopath and a narcissistic personality with no empathy for other people. It characterized him as a highly manipulative individual with an overwhelming need for control who wanted to be famous (or infamous) by leaving an indelible impression on the world. It stated that he also had sexual fantasies involving domination of women and deep-seated sadistic tendencies, as evidenced by his journal entries, which are seething with hatred for humanity. In contrast, Dylan Klebold suffered from a major depressive disorder with very low self-esteem and profound anger. He experienced suicidal ideation, had engaged in self-mutilation, and made numerous references in his journal to a sense of desperation and intense longing to be liberated from his despair. Special Agent Dr. Dwayne Fuselier, one of the key investigators, stated the following: "Because dyads, murderous pairs who feed off each other, account for only a fraction of mass murders, little research has been conducted on them. We know that the partnerships tend to be asymmetrical. An angry, erratic depressive and a sadistic psychopath make a combustible pair. The psychopath is in control, of course, but the hotheaded sidekick can sustain his excitement leading up to the big kill. It takes heat and cold to make a tornado."[97]

I have provided only a minuscule sample of mass shootings worldwide; I could have cited many more examples of this shocking phenomenon. I cannot help but wonder about a God who would allow so many thousands of people to be brutally murdered simply by being in the wrong place at the wrong time?

CHAPTER 8

Assorted Quotes and Humorous Tidbits

"I'm sort of an existential atheist. I believe that there is intelligent life on earth except in certain parts of New Jersey." - Woody Allen (American director, writer, actor, and comedian)

"I'm not afraid of death; I just don't want to be there when it happens." – Woody Allen

"To one who has faith, no explanation is necessary. To one without faith, no explanation is possible." - St. Thomas Aquinas (Italian Dominican friar, Catholic priest, and Doctor of the Church)

"We can't have full knowledge all at once. We must start by believing; then afterwards we may be led on to master the evidence for ourselves." – St. Thomas Aquinas

"The saddest aspect of life right now is that science gathers knowledge faster than society gathers wisdom." – Isaac

Asimov (Russian-born American author and biochemist who
wrote or edited nearly 500 books during his lifetime)

"Imagine the people who believe such things and who are not
ashamed to ignore, totally, all the patient findings of thinking
minds through all the centuries since the Bible was written.
And it is these ignorant people, the most uneducated, the most
unimaginative, the most unthinking among us, who would make
themselves the guides and leaders of us all; who would force their
feeble and childish beliefs on us; who would invade our schools and
libraries and homes. I personally resent it bitterly." – Isaac Asimov

"You can observe a lot just by watching." - Yogi
Berra (American baseball player)

"When you come to a fork in the road, take it." – Yogi Berra

"Three things cannot be long hidden: the sun, the moon,
and the truth. Just as a candle cannot burn without
fire, men cannot live without a spiritual life." - Buddha
(Philosopher, teacher, and religious leader whose
teachings formed the foundation of Buddhism)

"Health is the greatest gift, contentment the greatest
wealth, faithfulness the best relationship." – Buddha

"For if there is a sin against life, it consists perhaps not so
much in despairing of life as in hoping for another life
and in eluding the implacable grandeur of this life." -
Albert Camus (French philosopher, author, journalist,
and recipient of the Nobel Prize in Literature)

"I would rather live my life as if there is a God and die
to find out there isn't, than live as if there isn't and to
die to find out that there is." – Albert Camus

"If this is the best God can do, I am not impressed. Results like
these do not belong on the resume of a Supreme Being." - George
Carlin (American comedian, actor, author, and social critic)

"All the king's horses and all the king's men couldn't put
Humpty Dumpty back together again. That's because
there is no Humpty Dumpty, and there is no God. None,
not one, no God, never was." - George Carlin

"You don't go anywhere when you die. You just pass away. You
expire like a magazine subscription." - George Carlin

"Religion takes in billions of dollars; they pay no taxes,
and they always need a little more." - George Carlin

"Then there was the agnostic, dyslexic insomniac. He would lie
awake at night wondering if there's a DOG." - a clever person

"Yes, I know it's easy to make fun of the organized churches, but
has it occurred to anyone to wonder why it's so easy." – John
Cleese (British actor, comedian, screenwriter, and producer)

"If God did not intend for us to eat animals, then why
did he make them out of meat?" – John Cleese

"I am an agnostic because I am not afraid to think. I am not afraid
of any God in the universe who would send me or any other man

or woman to hell. If there were such a being, he would not be a God; he would be a devil." - Clarence Darrow (American lawyer and leading member of the American Civil Liberties Union)

"I do not consider it an insult, but rather a compliment to be called an agnostic. I do not pretend to know where many ignorant men are sure – that is all that agnosticism means." – Clarence Darrow

"The mystery of the beginning of all things is insoluble by us, and I for one must be content to remain an agnostic." - Charles Darwin (British naturalist, geologist, and biologist, best known for his contributions to the science of evolution)

"Ignorance more frequently begets confidence than does knowledge: it is those who know little, not those who know much, who so positively assert that this or that problem will never be solved by science." – Charles Darwin

"My eyes are constantly wide open to the extraordinary fact of existence. Not just human existence, but the existence of life and how this breathtakingly powerful process, which is natural selection, has managed to take the very simple facts of physics and chemistry and build them up to redwood trees and humans." - Richard Dawkins (British evolutionary biologist and author)

"Religion conditions people to believe that you do not have to support your beliefs with evidence." - Richard Dawkins

"We are all atheists about most of the gods that societies have ever believed in. Some of us just go one God further." - Richard Dawkins

"You can't even begin to understand biology, you can't understand life unless you understand what it's all there for, how it arose - and that means evolution." - Richard Dawkins

"The majority of children born into the world tend to inherit the beliefs of their parents, and that to me is one of the most regrettable facts of them all." - Richard Dawkins

"Many of us saw religion as harmless nonsense. Beliefs might lack all supporting evidence, but we thought if people needed a crutch for consolation, where's the harm? September 11th changed all that." - Richard Dawkins

"The take-home message is that we should blame religion itself, not religious extremism - as though that were some kind of terrible perversion of real, decent religion. Voltaire got it right long ago: 'Those who can make you believe absurdities can make you commit atrocities.' So did Bertrand Russell: 'Many people would sooner die than think. In fact, they do.'" - Richard Dawkins

"I have always considered 'Pascal's Wager' a questionable bet to place. Any God worth 'believing in' would surely prefer an honest agnostic to a calculating hypocrite." - Alan Dershowitz (American lawyer and scholar)

"It is the wall of separation between church and state that is largely responsible for religion thriving in this country, as compared to those European countries in which church and state have been united, resulting in opposition to the church by those who disapprove of the government." – Alan Dershowitz

"There are few things more dangerous than inbred religious certainty." – Bart D. Ehrman (American New Testament scholar focusing on textual criticism of the New Testament, the historical Jesus, and the origins and development of early Christianity)

"In Matthew, Jesus declares, 'Whoever is not with me is against me.' In Mark, he says, 'Whoever is not against us is for us.' Did he say both things? Could he mean both things? How can both be true at once? Or is it possible that one of the Gospel writers got things switched around?" - Bart D. Ehrman

"My position concerning God is that of an agnostic. I am convinced that a vivid consciousness of the primary importance of moral principles for the betterment and ennoblement of life does not need the idea of a law-giver, especially a law-giver who works on the basis of reward and punishment." Albert Einstein (German-Jewish theoretical physicist who developed the theory of relativity)

"Everything should be made as simple as possible;
but not simpler." - Albert Einstein

"God does not play dice with the universe." - Albert Einstein

"Imagination is more important than knowledge. Knowledge is limited. Imagination encircles the world." – Albert Einstein

"Unthinking respect for authority is the greatest enemy of truth." – Albert Einstein

"I believe in Spinoza's God who reveals himself in the orderly harmony of what exists, not in a God who concerns himself with the fates and actions of human beings." - Albert Einstein (Baruch Spinoza is generally considered to be the founder of scientific pantheism.)

"Religion is an illusion, and it derives its strength from the fact that it falls in with our instinctual desires." - Sigmund Freud (Austrian neurologist and founder of psychoanalysis)

"In the long run, nothing can withstand reason and experience, and the contradiction religion offers to both is palpable." – Sigmund Freud

"The great question that has never been answered, and which I have not yet been able to answer, despite my thirty years of research into the feminine soul, is: 'What does a woman want?'" – Sigmund Freud

"In terms of doing things, I take a fairly scientific approach as to why things happen and how they happen. I don't know if there's a God or not." - Bill Gates (American billionaire and co-founder of the Microsoft Corporation)

"Success is a lousy teacher. It seduces smart people into thinking they can't lose." – Bill Gates

"I sentence you to an eternity in hell for committing the unpardonable sin of being intellectually honest with yourself and other people." - God (a message to all non-Christians)

"I am a Roman Catholic and a Buddhist (joint enrollment)." - Michael Grost (American mathematician and software designer with a tested IQ of approximately 200)

"What I'm asking you to entertain is that there is nothing we need to believe on insufficient evidence in order to have deeply ethical and spiritual lives." - Sam Harris (American author, neuroscientist, and philosopher)

"Just think of the Muslims who are blowing themselves up convinced that they are agents of God's will." - Sam Harris

"I know of no society in human history that ever suffered because it's people became too desirous of evidence in support of their core beliefs." - Sam Harris

"We are each free to believe what we want, and it is my view that the simplest explanation is there is no God. No one created the universe, and no one directs our fate. This leads me to a profound realization. There is probably no heaven and no afterlife either. We have this one life to appreciate the grand design of the universe, and for that, I am extremely grateful." - Dr. Stephen Hawking (British theoretical physicist, cosmologist, and author who was Director of Research at the Centre for Theoretical Cosmology at the University of Cambridge)

"So, when people ask me if a God created the universe, I tell them that the question itself makes no sense. Time didn't exist before the Big Bang, so there is no time for God to make the universe in. It's like asking for directions to the edge of the earth. The earth is a sphere. It doesn't have an edge, so looking for it is a futile exercise." - Dr. Stephen Hawking

"Thus, though I dislike to differ with such a great man, Voltaire was simply ludicrous when he said that if God did not exist, it would be necessary to invent him. The human invention of God is the problem to begin with." - Christopher Hitchens (British-American author, journalist, and social critic)

"Violent, irrational, intolerant, allied to racism and tribalism and bigotry, invested in ignorance and hostile to free inquiry, contemptuous of women and coercive toward children; organized religion ought to have a great deal on its conscience." - Christopher Hitchens

"I know of no wars started by anyone to impose lack of religion on someone else. We have lethal Sunni vs. Shia, Catholic against Protestant, but no agnostic suicide bombers attack crowded atheist pubs." – Simon Hoggart (British journalist and broadcaster who wrote about politics for *The Guardian*)

"What has always puzzled me is the flexibility of God's word. For instance, Catholics can now eat meat on Fridays. And limbo has been abolished. How does this work? Who tells them?" – Simon Hoggart

"If God is omnipotent, omniscient, and wholly good, whence evil? If God wills to prevent evil but cannot, then He is not omnipotent. If He can prevent evil but does not, then He is not good. In either case, he is not God." – David Hume (Scottish philosopher, historian, and economist)

"Nothing is more surprising than the easiness with which
the many are governed by the few." – David Hume

"For the first time in the history of the world, Buddhism proclaimed
a salvation which each individual could gain from him or herself,
in this world, during this life, without any least reference to
God, or to gods either great or small." - Aldous Huxley (English
novelist, best noted for his classic work *Brave New World*)

"That men do not learn very much from the lessons
of history is the most important of all the lessons
that history has to teach." – Aldous Huxley

"Maybe this world is another planet's hell." – Aldous Huxley

"If a man would follow, today, the teachings of the Old
Testament, he would be a criminal. If he would follow strictly
the teachings of the New, he would be insane." – Robert G.
Ingersoll (American lawyer, orator, and noted agnostic)

"Our government should be entirely and purely
secular. The religious views of a candidate should be
kept entirely out of sight." - Robert G. Ingersoll

"If every trace of any single religion were wiped out and nothing
were passed on, it would never be created exactly that way
again. There might be some other nonsense in its place, but not
that exact nonsense. If all of science were wiped out, it would
still be true, and someone would find a way to figure it all out
again." – Penn Jillette (American magician, actor, musician,
inventor, television personality, and best-selling author)

"You get no moral credit for forcing other people to do what you think is right." – Penn Jillette

"I believe that the best way to become an atheist is to read the Bible." – Penn Jillette

"Always recognize that human individuals are ends, and do not use them as means to your end." – Immanuel Kant (German philosopher and one of the most influential figures in modern Western philosophy)

"He who is cruel to animals becomes hard also in his dealings with men. We can judge the heart of a man by his treatment of animals." – Immanuel Kant

"Life can only be understood backwards; but it must be lived forwards." - Soren Kierkegaard (Danish philosopher, poet, and religious author who is regarded by some as the first existentialist philosopher)

"I found I had less and less to say, until finally, I became silent, and began to listen. I discovered in the silence, the voice of God." - Soren Kierkegaard

"I believe that robots are stealing my luggage." - Steve Martin (American comedian, actor, and musician)

"Thankfully, persistence is a great substitute for talent." – Steve Martin

"Religion is the sigh of the oppressed creature, the heart of a heartless world, and the soul of soulless conditions. It is the opium of the people." - Karl Marx (German philosopher, economist, and historian)

"Religion is the impotence of the human mind to deal with occurrences it cannot understand." – Karl Marx

"I refuse to join any club that would have me as a member." - Groucho Marx (American comedian and actor)

"Well, I tell you, if I have been wrong in my agnosticism, when I die, I'll walk up to God in a manly way and say, Sir, I made an honest mistake." - H.L. Mencken (German American satirist, social critic, and freethinker)

"Moral certainty is always a sign of cultural inferiority. The more uncivilized the man, the surer he is that he knows precisely what is right and what is wrong. All human progress, even in morals, has been the work of men who have doubted the current moral values, not of men who have whooped them up and tried to enforce them. The truly civilized man is always skeptical and tolerant in this field as in all others. His culture is based on: 'I am not too sure.'" – H.L. Mencken

"The government consists of a gang of men exactly like you and me. They have, taking one with another, no special talent for the business of government; they have only a talent for getting and holding office. Their principal device to that end is to search out groups who pant and pine for something they can't get and to promise to give it to them. Nine times

out of ten that promise is worth nothing. The tenth time
is made good by looting A to satisfy B. In other words,
government is a broker in pillage, and every election is sort of
an advance auction sale of stolen goods." – H.L. Mencken

"Nobody gets out alive." - Jim Morrison
(frontman for the rock band *The Doors*)

"This is the strangest life I have ever known." – Jim Morrison

"God is dead. God remains dead. And we have killed him. Yet his
shadow still looms. How shall we comfort ourselves, the murderers
of all murderers? What was holiest and mightiest of all that the
world has yet owned has bled to death under our knives; who
will wipe this blood off us? What water is there for us to clean
ourselves?" – Friedrich Nietzsche (German philosopher, cultural
critic, composer, poet, philologist, and Latin and Greek scholar)

"The individual has always had to struggle to keep from being
overwhelmed by the tribe. If you try it, you will be lonely often,
and sometimes frightened. But no price is too high to pay for
the privilege of owning yourself." – Friedrich Nietzsche

"Of all the systems of religion that ever were invented, there
is no more derogatory to the Almighty, more unedifying to
man, more repugnant to reason, and more contradictory to
itself than this thing called Christianity." - Thomas Paine
(British-born American philosopher and political activist)

"All national institutions of churches, whether Jewish,
Christian, or Turkish, appear to me no other than human

inventions set up to terrify and enslave mankind, and
monopolize power and profit." - Thomas Paine

"Belief is a wise wager. Granted that faith cannot be proved, what
harm will come to you if you gamble on its truth, and it proves
false? If you gain, you gain all; if you lose, you lose nothing.
Wager, then without hesitation, that He exists." – Blaise Pascal
(French mathematician, writer, and Catholic theologian)

"Men never commit evil so fully and joyfully as when
they do it for religious convictions." – Blaise Pascal

"As to the gods, I have no means of knowing either that they
exist or that they do not exist, nor what sort of form they may
have; there are many reasons why knowledge on this subject is
not possible, owing to the lack of evidence and the shortness
of human life." - Protagoras (ancient Greek philosopher)

"Man is the measure of all things: of things which are, that they
are, and of things which are not, that they are not." – Protagoras

"When I die, I hope to go to heaven, whatever the hell that is."
- Ayn Rand (Russian-American author and philosopher)

"Devotion to the truth is the hallmark of morality; there is no
greater, nobler, more heroic form of devotion than the act of a
man who assumes the responsibility of thinking." – Ayn Rand

"The truth is not for all men but only for
those who seek it." – Ayn Rand

"The prayer of the agnostic: 'O God, if there is a God, save my soul if I have a soul.'" – Ernest Renan (French philosopher, biblical scholar, and historian of religion)

"None of the miracles with which ancient histories are filled occurred under scientific conditions. Observation never once contradicted, teaches us that miracles occur only in periods and countries in which they are believed in and before persons disposed to believe in them." – Ernest Renan

"It is possible that mankind is on the threshold of a golden age: but, if so, it will be necessary first to slay the dragon that guards the door, and this dragon is religion." – Bertrand Russell (British philosopher, mathematician, historian, and political activist)

"As soon as we abandon our own reason and are content to rely upon authority, there is no end to our troubles." - Bertrand Russell

"And if there were a God, I think it very unlikely that He would have such an uneasy vanity as to be offended by those who doubt His existence." – Bertrand Russell

"The Cosmos is all that is or ever was or ever will be." - Carl Sagan (American astronomer and author)

"Cosmos is a Greek word for the order of the universe. It is, in a way, the opposite of chaos. It implies the deep interconnectedness of all things. It conveys awe for the intricate and subtle way in which the universe is put together." - Carl Sagan

"Life has no meaning a priori…It is up to you to give it a meaning, and value is nothing but the meaning that you choose." – Jean-Paul Sartre (French existentialist philosopher, playwright, novelist, screenwriter, political activist, and literary critic)

"If you are lonely when you're alone, you are in bad company." – Jean-Paul Sartre

"All great truths begin as blasphemies." – George Bernard Shaw (Irish playwright, critic, and political activist)

"The fact that a believer is happier than a skeptic is no more to the point than the fact that a drunken man is happier than a sober one." – George Bernard Shaw

"True wisdom comes to each of us when we realize how little we understand about life, ourselves, and the world around us." – Socrates (classical Greek philosopher considered to be one of the founders of Western philosophy)

"By all means, marry. If you get a good wife, you'll become happy; if you get a bad one, you'll become a philosopher." – Socrates

"The holy word of God is on everyone's lips…but…we see almost everyone presenting their own versions of God's word, with the sole purpose of using religion as a pretext for making others think as they do." – Baruch Spinoza (Jewish-Dutch philosopher considered one of the great rationalists of 17th-century philosophy)

"He who regulates everything by laws is more likely to arouse vices than reform them." - Baruch Spinoza

"What one man calls God, another calls the laws of physics." – Nikola Tesla (Serbian-American inventor, electrical engineer, and futurist who is best known for his contributions to the design of the modern alternating current electricity supply system)

"The day science begins to study non-physical phenomena, it will make more progress in one decade than in all the previous centuries of its existence." – Nikola Tesla

"The Bible has noble poetry in it...and some good morals and a wealth of obscenity, and upwards of a thousand lies." - Mark Twain (American writer and humorist)

"It is better to keep your mouth closed and let people think you are a fool than to open it and remove all doubt." - Mark Twain

"If you tell the truth, you don't have to remember anything." – Mark Twain

"A lie can travel halfway around the world while the truth is putting on its shoes." - Mark Twain

"What people are really after is, what is my stance on religion or spirituality or God? And I would say, if I find a word that came closest, it would be agnostic." – Neil deGrasse Tyson (American astrophysicist, author, and television personality)

"The universe is under no obligation to make sense to you." – Neil deGrasse Tyson

"I once wanted to become an atheist, but I gave up – they
have no holidays." – Henny Youngman (American comedian
and musician. Known as "King of the One-Liners")

"If God did not exist it would be necessary to invent him." - Voltaire
(French Enlightenment writer, historian, and philosopher)

"Life is a shipwreck, but we must not forget
to sing in the lifeboats." – Voltaire

"Religion is like a blind man looking in a black
room for a black cat that isn't there and finding
it." – Oscar Wilde (Irish poet and playwright)

"Experience is merely the name men gave
to their mistakes." – Oscar Wilde

CHAPTER 9

Quotes from Yours Truly: More Humorous Tidbits

I dread the wrath of God, especially if there is a God.

As a Catholic, agnostic Buddhist, I agree
with everyone about everything.

You can go over to Africa and watch babies starve to death
before they reach the age of five. If that somehow fits into
God's Divine Plan, then I'm just at a loss for words.

I would hate to think of Dr. Stephen Hawking, an atheist, burning
in hell forever. He was a brilliant, kindly man who was trapped
in a wheelchair for most of his life, so it just doesn't seem fair
that God would cast him into hell. However, if Dr. Hawking
is in hell, I wonder if they let him keep his wheelchair.

At some point, my tick-tocker is going to stop tick-tocking.
As far as what happens after that, I have no idea.

After God created the universe and saw all the wickedness humankind was capable of, he said the following: "D'OH!"

I used to go to an agnostic church, and the sermon was always the same. The pastor would stand at the pulpit and say: "Hey, I don't know. Does anybody here have the answer? No? Okay, let's all go eat."

I don't want to be involved in the Rapture because I have a fear of heights.

The universe is incredible in and of itself, and there doesn't have to be anything beyond it.

How about those dopey Buddhists worshiping a pot-bellied, little Chinaman sitting there with a self-satisfied grin on his face? The same goes for the Hindus worshiping a statue with twenty-seven arms and legs. The Christian God is a loving grandfather figure with white hair, a white beard, and a flowing white robe. He's probably about two hundred feet tall, and I bet that He could beat up Godzilla.

The only thing I'm certain about is that I'm not certain about anything.

I wouldn't be so paranoid if everyone weren't out to get me.

Immanuel Kant, but at least he tries.

One Sunday, I felt kind of Catholic after leaving Mass. I guess I just got swept up by the pageantry of it all. But cooler heads prevailed, and by the afternoon, I was agnostic again. One thing I don't understand is the ridiculous hats those guys wear. I feel like I'm at a gay Halloween party.

I think that maybe I should fly over to France and visit the sacred shrine of Lourdes. That's where the Blessed Mother supposedly appeared to a 14-year-old peasant girl named Bernadette Soubirous in a series of apparitions. In one of them, she instructed Bernadette to dig into the ground with her hands, after which water came mysteriously bubbling out. Over the years, people with horrible maladies bathed in the waters of Lourdes, and some of them claim to have been miraculously healed. Hey, who knows, it might be true! If the French could idolize Jerry Lewis, then I say that anything is possible. Just kidding, Jerry Lewis was a great entertainer and humanitarian.

Well, if it turns out that Christianity is true, then I guess I'll be cast into hell along with Bill Gates and Warren Buffet, two of the most generous philanthropists who ever lived. The worst part is that they won't be able to give me any money down there, and even if they could, there would be nothing to spend it on.

I'm somewhat confused by the French philosopher/mathematician Blaise Pascal. His famous wager certainly sounds like the words of an agnostic, yet he is regarded as a defender of Christianity. From my point of view, that flies in the face of reason.

When Christian preachers get caught in some scandal, they typically deliver a passionate apology pleading with their supporters to please forgive their sin and let them move on. They shed enough crocodile tears to fill an Olympic size swimming pool.

Christian TV preachers always have something to sell, like their latest book or CD series, that you absolutely must have in your library. I thought that the Bible, the alleged word of God, is all that we need. Christians can read their Bible every day, join a Bible study group at their church, and have everything they need for salvation. They don't need to buy the latest book or CD course from some millionaire preachers.

I've had discussions with some believers whose argument for God's existence runs as follows: "There are many good people in the world; therefore, God exists." How so many reasonably intelligent people can make this leap of logic is beyond me.

Suicide is a courageous act, and I do not dare to commit suicide other than under the direction of a physician when I'm terminally ill. I firmly believe that we should legalize physician-assisted suicide in America. To force a person with a terminal illness to suffer until the bitter end in the final stage of their life constitutes cruel and unusual punishment, in my opinion.

I'm tired of people using the words "awesome" and "incredible" to describe various things when these terms are entirely inappropriate. Most things in life are not awesome or incredible; they are merely average and boring.

I can no longer watch commercials on television nor listen to them on the radio. I understand that companies have to advertise their products and services, but I simply cannot stand them anymore. Usually, they involve things that I have no interest in, and I feel they are just wasting my time.

The deification of professional athletes in America is entirely misguided, in my view. These are exceptionally gifted people regarding their athletic ability, but they are not eminent philosophers or social commentators whose every word we should hang on.

The secret to success is sincerity. Once you can fake that, you've got it made.

Companies should stop saying that our safety is their top priority, which is nothing more than Orwellian doublespeak. Their top priority is profit, and that's fine. I just wish they would stop lying about it.

Sports is mostly the truth, but politics is mostly a lie.

I can't seem to escape the sneaking suspicion that America is turning into a nation of fat slobs, alcoholics, drug addicts, and perverts. I hope that I'm wrong, but that does not appear to be the case.

It seems that the national media cannot resist the urge to editorialize while presenting the news. One gets the impression that the press can psychically divine our political leaders' intentions and motives, a journalistic sixth sense, if you will.

Why do people speak of "Mother Nature"? What's maternal about nature, especially when it's killing thousands of people with natural disasters?

I don't think that I would recognize happiness even if it came up and bit me on the butt! The best that I can hope for is contentment, a feeling of being relatively satisfied with my current status in life.

Many people simply slide through life on the surface of reality. They never do any meaningful research about any subject, nor do they ever think deeply about anything, so they don't have any real depth of understanding.

One nice thing about being a pessimist is that once in a while, I'm pleasantly surprised.

A person cannot possess any more than 1/1000 of a percent of the total fund of human knowledge accumulated over time. Thus, I find it both amusing and somewhat annoying when people behave arrogantly due to their supposedly vast storehouse of knowledge.

People interrupt me so often that it doesn't even bother me anymore. Most of the time, they're not rude; they just feel the need to respond to me as soon as they understand what I'm saying. Perhaps this is because many people are so pressed for time nowadays.

I enjoy the rain, and I love thunderstorms— especially at night. I find the sound of rain to be comforting, a break in the monotony of life.

Years ago, I was friends with a brilliant man who had been Texas State Chess Champion. I once asked his opinion regarding the meaning of life, and he replied, "Oh, life. Well, life is just something to do."

Who came up with the idea that the heart has something to do with human emotion? The heart is an organ that pumps blood throughout the body via the circulatory system, which serves to supply oxygen and nutrients to the tissues and to remove carbon dioxide and other waste material. The heart has absolutely nothing to do with emotion. When someone says that he feels something deep in his heart, he might just be having gas.

In my opinion, one of the greatest movies ever made is *Godzilla: King of The Monsters* starring Raymond Burr as newspaper correspondent Steve Martin. I can just picture him crawling out of the wreckage of Tokyo with an arrow in his head.

In the words of the great Leonardo da Vinci: "Mona, will you please sit still and wipe that stupid grin off your face!"

In my younger years, I had a fixation with the female anatomy combined with a sincere love of red wine, which led me into various establishments where women dance professionally, if you catch my drift.

I once read an article about Iceland, one of the safest countries globally and relatively low on the scale of religiosity. It stated that there had been fewer homicides in Iceland throughout the entire twentieth century than there are in the United States in one day. Despite the enormous difference in population, I find that fact to be mind-boggling. What a dangerous, violent country America seems to have become!

Didn't Jesus say that those who live by the sword die by the sword? It seems to me that many people who have not lived by

the sword die by the sword anyway as victims of genocide, mass
shootings, and other heinous crimes. Nothing against Jesus;
I'm just trying to bring some balance to the conversation.

Didn't Jesus also say that if someone strikes you on the
cheek, you should turn the other cheek and let him strike
you there, as well? Pardon my confusion, but that seems
like an excellent way to get smacked around a lot.

Modern American capitalism will take every penny you have
and leave you face down in a gutter if you allow it to do so. All-
day long, we are bombarded with wall-to-wall advertising for
a vast spectacle of products and services, many of which we
can't afford and don't need. For this reason, there needs to be
financial education in which we teach people to be very prudent
with their money lest they wind up in a hopeless predicament.

If God is all-powerful and outraged by abortion, why have
there been over 60 million abortions in the United States
since Roe vs. Wade in 1973? When does God finally get fed
up and say enough is enough? When does He finally put
his foot down? Here's another question: If sensuality is so
evil, why do tornados never seem to hit topless bars?

I sometimes hear people say that America is still the
greatest country in the world. Everyone is entitled to
their opinion, but my vote goes to Switzerland.

If a sadist loves to torture people and a masochist loves
to be tortured, then wouldn't a sadist be torturing
a masochist by refusing to torture him?

As the Bible clearly states: "Verily, verily I say unto thee, it is forbidden to breaketh wind on the Sabbath." (I'm paraphrasing)

Here's a fun fact: There is an island off the coast of Brazil called Ilha da Queimada Grande, also known as "Snake Island." It is inhabited by as many as 5,000 highly venomous snakes; a unique pit viper called the golden lancehead. The island is off-limits to the general public by order of the Brazilian Navy. It is widely considered to be the most dangerous place on earth, with the possible exception of East St. Louis.

Why do we keep hearing about massive lawsuits against pharmaceutical companies? I thought these companies spend millions of dollars testing their new drugs and getting approval from the Food and Drug Administration. Is the FDA just another government scam?

The English language is a wondrous and mysterious thing. Why else would so many gifted people have devoted their lives to it?

I'll probably die with rosary beads in my hands and my middle finger pointed skyward.

In the evening, I like to play chess on the internet and drink red wine. Of course, the quality of my play tends to decline as the evening progresses.

I read that Jesus drove evil spirits out of a crazy man and into a bunch of pigs, who ran down a hill into the sea where they drowned. Doesn't that constitute animal cruelty? I think that PETA would have a big problem with this story.

Always remember the words of timekeepers at track and
field events: "These are the souls that time men's tries."

Remember this valuable advice if you are hiking in bear
country. If you see a mama grizzly bear with her
cubs, be sure to walk right up to her and play with
the cubs. This shows mama that you're friendly.

Let's face it. We've all made mistakes in this life.
Nobody's perfect, as the Elephant Man once said.

One way to reduce poverty in America is to reduce the
number of poor people by paying them not to reproduce.
Hopefully, by doing this, we can alleviate the generational
curse of poverty which plagues many people.

A military firing squad should publicly execute people who
abuse children or animals, and we should televise it.

Pastor John Hagee of the Cornerstone Church in San Antonio,
Texas, has stated that a person who does not work should not
eat. When the US economy is reasonably healthy, we typically
have an unemployment rate of about four to five percent, a
figure representing millions of people. I suppose that Pastor
Hagee would advocate that all of those people should starve
to death rather than receive help from relatives or government
assistance to get them through a difficult period in their lives.
This guy has about as much compassion as a rabid pit bull.

Why bother with the Infinite Regress when you can just go with
the simplest explanation that there is perhaps no God at all?

We need to have law and order even if there is no God.
Otherwise, criminals would take over the world.

I think organized religion may be a complete scam that evil men
created for the sole purpose of separating people from their money.

If a pantheist feels better by calling himself a pantheist rather
than an atheist, that's fine with me. However, if you don't
acknowledge some transcendent, creative force beyond the
universe, then as far as I'm concerned, you're an atheist.

When I was a little kid, I thought that God's name
was Harold because I thought it was: "Our Father
who art in heaven, Harold be thy name."

How could it be the case that the Roman Catholic Church
would be embroiled in an enormous scandal due to the
sexual crimes of some Catholic priests? What kind of
God would allow so many people to be horribly abused
and completely disillusioned with their faith?

Someone once said that we should be allowed to do
our life repeatedly until we get it right. My question
is: How will we know when we get it right?

The only miracle that I'm aware of is the
miracle of compound interest.

I have two guardian angels. Their names are Smith and Wesson.

So, Albert Einstein missed the boat as an agnostic, but the Catholic nuns had it all figured out. As the Bible suggests, "Givest thou unto me a freakin' break!"

To those fraudulent Christian preachers who enrich themselves at the expense of their gullible followers (and you know who you are), you are all loathsome maggots; you should be forced to return every penny you have stolen and spend the rest of your miserable lives in prison.

What's the point of having regret? Each of us could have gone down thousands of different paths in life, and there's absolutely no way of knowing how any other course would have turned out. So, there's no point in having regret. Screw regret!

What is the truth? The truth is that the truth is unknowable.

Someone who knew that I'm an agnostic once said to me: "How can you look at a smiling baby and not believe in God?" I responded: "How can you look at a baby that's dying of cancer and believe in God?" The conversation came to a rapid conclusion.

One thing that's amazing to me is the hostility that some Christians express toward atheists and agnostics. It's as if we spend all of our waking hours torturing kittens. I don't feel any animosity toward Christians; I just tend to disagree with them.

I think that churches should be required to pay a small amount of their annual income in the form of taxes, maybe five to ten percent. Any bozo can start his own church, pay himself a salary, and start taking donations. Individuals and corporations have to pay taxes to the federal government, so why should churches get off scot-free?

Am I to believe that some awesome God communicated with Adam and Eve in the Garden of Eden, but then some snake came slithering along and persuaded Eve to eat from the tree of forbidden fruit? That snake must have been one hell of a salesman.

The fact that life is filled with pain and disappointment does not imply, in the least, that there is some sort of blissful euphoria waiting for us in the next life. There is no connection between the two.

The Protestants have heaven and hell, and the Catholics threw in purgatory to give people false hope. You can also buy your loved ones out of purgatory with a few bucks, which was a big reason for the Protestant Reformation in the first place.

If anyone can convince me that agnosticism is not the most intellectually honest position to take, I'll eat my hat. Fortunately, I do not own a hat.

Here is the epitaph on the tombstone of playwright George Bernard Shaw: "I knew if I hung around long enough, something like this would happen!"

So, every non-Christian who has ever lived and has passed on is now burning in hell for eternity. They are writhing in unceasing agony. I must confess that I have a big problem with that concept.

I heard there was a fourth wise man, and he was supposed to bring the potato salad, but he got lost and ate it all himself.

I doubt that the Jews are the chosen people of God since there may not even be a God, and I am not waiting for the imminent return of Jesus Christ since he may never have existed either. If that's blasphemy, then I guess I'm guilty of blasphemy.

When I reflect on all the pain that this world has endured, it leads me to imagine that we might just have the Marquis de Sade up there in heaven.

I sometimes wonder why I am me as opposed to being someone else. Nobody has a vote before their birth as to what they are going to be. Probably everyone would vote to be extremely intelligent, good-looking, and talented, so I guess it's just not realistic to allow people to have a say in the matter.

All in all, I don't feel cheated by life since I had a lot of fun. What about an eighteen-year-old kid who signed up to serve in the military during World War II? They send him over to Normandy to participate in the D-Day invasion, and he drowns on the way to the beach, where he might have gotten shot to death anyway. That's what I would call being cheated by life. At least I never had to serve in the military, so I never got shot in some horrible war.

I disagree with those existentialists who claim that life is absurd. They say that we just are born, go through school, get a job, get married, have a few kids, and then get old and die—unless we die young. After that, the universe doesn't skip a beat. The universe doesn't miss us at all. We are nothing more than ornaments in the universe. However, if you say that life is absurd, I must pose the question: What is absurdity? Well, absurdity is the contradiction of meaning. To have absurdity, there must be some identifiable meaning that's being contradicted. However, life is the totality of our existence, so you cannot get outside of life to view it from a third-party vantage point. It is impossible to create a contrast between the absurdity of life and the meaningfulness of something other than life. Therefore, the statement that life is absurd is logically untenable, in my opinion.

If you send a letter to God in Jerusalem, Israel, it gets placed into the Wailing Wall, where Jewish people pray every day. Well, I did that a long time ago, and I asked God for some relief from this annoying tinnitus that I suffer with, and not a damn thing happened.

I am an agnostic and a Libertarian. I think that we should end this ridiculous drug war immediately. Prohibition was the greatest thing that ever happened to organized crime, and now we're doing it all over again. In America, we lock up non-violent drug offenders while allowing vicious murderers and child molesters to serve life in prison where they get three meals a day at taxpayer expense. What is wrong with this picture?

I talk to myself all the time. That way, I never get an argument.

How about Albert Einstein with all his wacky theories?! What kind of drugs was that guy doing? "Mass expands as it approaches the speed of light"!? Dude, gimme a hit on that joint. I can't believe they made a bomb out of that!

I don't think that parents should spend a great deal of time drumming the idea of a God and religion into their child's head. Instead, they should continually emphasize the importance of developing strong, marketable skills. After the child graduates from college or technical school, he can immediately begin on his career path rather than moving back in with Mom and Dad while struggling under a mountain of student loan debt.

If there is a place called heaven and I somehow manage to go there, I hope they have an infinite supply of Snickers Bars, Reese's Peanut Butter Cups, and Hostess Fruit Pies. Also, expensive red wine from the private collection of Robert Mondavi. He once called me just to say thanks for my support.

After I die, I would like to become an angel with a huge rottweiler named Bobo. God would place me in different situations where someone is about to be assaulted. I would command the assailant to leave the scene immediately and, if he does not comply, then I would have Bobo tear him to shreds. Then I would accompany the intended victim to his or her destination, after which Bobo and I would disappear right before their eyes. I could really get into that.

The best time to become a drug addict is when you're dying.

I'm glad that I never had kids because my kids would have been short like me, and short people have no reason to live. Just ask Randy Newman.

Some might say that I'm an atheist masquerading as an agnostic, but I'm really an agnostic masquerading as a Catholic.

A friend of mine once asked me if I consider myself a normal person or an abnormal person. I asked him what it means to be a normal person, and he could not answer the question. I have no idea whether I'm a normal or an abnormal person.

God gives us guys this massive libido where we want to screw anything that moves but then tells us that we must crucify our flesh. Will you please make up your mind?

My version of heaven would be to wake up on the morning of September 6th, 1956—my fourth birthday—knowing everything that I know now. On the other hand, maybe I'd just completely screw it up all over again.

Doesn't the Bible say what God has joined together, let no man tear asunder, referring to the institution of marriage? Well, now we have a fifty percent divorce rate in America, so it seems to me that God is about as powerful as a Nevada boxing commissioner.

Didn't Jesus say, "Blessed are they who have not seen and yet believe"? According to that logic, I could believe in anything that I have not seen, like leprechauns, or unicorns, or Eskimos. Oh wait, I have seen Eskimos.

It's impossible to do anything right away because right away is already gone.

If I had to put money on it, I would say that I will simply cease to exist when I die. Of course, that's a bet that I can never collect on.

Let's focus on creating a better world for everyone rather than wasting a lot of time worshiping an Invisible Man in the Sky.

For me, the bottom line is this: Even if there is no God, even if no one created the universe, at least I did the best that I could in this world, based on my changing perception of reality. That may be a small consolation, but it's the only consolation I have.

Writing this book has made me acutely aware of just how abysmally ignorant I am. We can only scratch the surface of the total fund of human knowledge, which is increasing at an extraordinary rate. Hopefully, this will lead to a higher quality of life for all of us, including animals.

In closing, let me say that, throughout your life, you have to make various decisions. Some of them will be more or less automatic, like when you're driving in traffic. You have to make decisions pretty quickly in these situations, but it's usually fairly obvious as to what the correct decision is. Other decisions require much more thought and research, such as deciding what the best career path is, what investments to make with your available resources, where you want to live, who you want to marry, or if you're going to get married. These are significant decisions that can profoundly affect the quality of your life.

My advice is to be as thorough as you can in evaluating your options and seeking advice from people you trust. The internet is a useful resource in this regard. However, even if you do detailed analysis and seek advice from wise, experienced people you respect, you may still feel that you made the wrong decision. Such is the random cruelty of life. If it turns out that you later think you made the wrong decision, do not, I repeat, DO NOT allow yourself to be crippled with regret. Regret is an insidious trap that can destroy your life if you allow it to do so. Instead, you must evaluate your current circumstances and make the best decision that you can with the methodology I have outlined. It comes down to rolling with the punches and dealing with the unfortunate events that life sometimes metes out. Good luck, and may you have a happy, prosperous life in this random, perplexing world.

APPENDIX

Some Noted Agnostics

Saul Alinsky (1909-1972) was an American community organizer and author. He is best remembered for his book *Rules for Radicals.*

Poul Anderson (1926-2001) was an American science fiction author.

Piers Anthony (born 1934) is a British-American writer of science fiction and fantasy.

Susan B. Anthony (1820-1906) was an American civil rights leader who played a major role in the women's rights movement of the 19th century and who helped women to gain the right to vote in the United States.

Hannah Arendt (1906-1975) was a German American philosopher and political theorist.

Samuel Beckett (1906-1989) was an Irish playwright, novelist, poet, and theater director. He was the recipient of the Nobel Prize in Literature in 1969.

Alexander Graham Bell (1847-1922) was a Scottish-born scientist, inventor, and engineer who invented and patented the first practical telephone. He founded the American Telephone and Telegraph Company in 1885.

Tom Bergeron (born 1955) is a popular television personality and game show host. He has hosted *America's Funniest Home Videos*, *Hollywood Squares*, and *Dancing with the Stars*.

Ingmar Bergman (1918-2007) was a highly regarded Swedish director, writer, and producer. He is generally considered one of the most gifted and influential filmmakers of all time. His films include such masterpieces as *Smiles of a Summer Night*, *The Seventh Seal*, *Wild Strawberries*, and *Cries and Whispers*.

Irving Berlin (1888-1989) was an American composer often regarded as one of the greatest songwriters in American history.

Ambrose Bierce (1842-circa 1914) was a satirist, journalist, and short-story writer. He is best known for his humorous work, *The Devil's Dictionary*.

Lewis Black (born 1948) is an American comedian, author, playwright, and social critic.

Jorge Luis Borges (1899-1986) was an Argentine short-story writer, essayist, poet, and translator.

Johannes Brahms (1833-1897) was a German composer and pianist. He is regarded as one of "The Three B's," along with J.S. Bach and Ludwig Van Beethoven.

Warren Buffett (born 1930) is an American billionaire investor and CEO of Berkshire Hathaway. He is also one of the leading philanthropists in the world, along with Bill Gates.

Henry Cadbury (1883-1974) was an American biblical scholar, Quaker historian, writer, and non-profit administrator.

Thomas Carlyle (1795-1881) was a Scottish writer and historian during the Victorian era.

Dick Cavett (born 1936) is an American television talk show host.

Charlie Chaplin (1889-1977) was an English comedic actor during the silent film era.

Confucius (551-479 BC) was a highly influential Chinese teacher, politician, and philosopher. His ideas were later developed into a Chinese religious system known as Confucianism.

Aaron Copland (1900-1990) was an American composer, writer, and conductor. He is best known for his compositions "Appalachian Spring," "Fanfare for the Common Man," and "The Tender Land."

Francis Crick (1916-2004) was a British molecular biologist, biophysicist, and neuroscientist. He was a co-discoverer of the structure of DNA with James Watson. He described himself as an agnostic with a strong inclination toward atheism.

Marie Curie (1867-1934) was a Polish physicist, chemist, and pioneer in the study of radioactivity. She was the first woman to win a Nobel Prize and the first person to win two Nobel Prizes in two different sciences: the Nobel Prize in Physics in 1903 and the Nobel Prize in Chemistry in 1911.

Clarence Darrow (1857-1938) was an American lawyer and a prominent member of the American Civil Liberties Union. He is noted for defending John T. Scopes, a substitute high school teacher, in the famous Scopes Monkey Trial.

Charles Darwin (1809-1892) was a British biologist, geologist, and naturalist. He is best known for his work in the development of the science of evolution.

John Dewey (1859-1952) was an American philosopher and psychologist whose ideas were influential in education and social reform.

Leonardo DiCaprio (born 1974) is an American actor, film producer, and environmentalist. He has been nominated for six Academy Awards, four British Academy Film Awards, and nine Screen Actors Guild Awards and has won one of each award as well as three Golden Globe Awards.

Ariel Dorfman (born 1942) is an Argentine/Chilean/American novelist, playwright, and essayist.

Sir Arthur Conan Doyle (1859-1930) was a Scottish writer who is best known for his stories about the famous detective Sherlock Holmes. He also wrote science fiction stories, plays, poetry, and historical novels.

Richard Dreyfuss (born 1947) is an American actor best known for his roles in *Jaws, American Graffiti, Stand by Me, Close Encounters of the Third Kind,* and *The Goodbye Girl.* He received an Academy Award for Best Actor in 1978 for his role in *The Goodbye Girl.*

W.E.B. Du Bois (1868-1963) was an American sociologist, historian, civil rights activist, and author. He was also a co-founder of the National Association for the Advancement of Colored People (NAACP) in 1909.

Émile Durkheim (1858-1917) was a French sociologist considered one of the primary founders of modern social science. He was raised

Jewish, briefly flirted with Catholicism after an allegedly mystical experience, and later became an agnostic.

Bart D. Ehrman (born 1955) is an American New Testament scholar focusing on textual criticism of the New Testament, the historical Jesus, and the origins and development of early Christianity. He has written and edited thirty books, including three college textbooks and six New York Times bestsellers.

Albert Einstein (1879-1955) was a German-Jewish theoretical physicist who developed the theory of relativity—one of the two foundations of modern physics.

Enrico Fermi (1901-1954) was an Italian American physicist and the creator of the world's first nuclear reactor: the Chicago Pile-1. He is noted for his enormous contributions to theoretical physics and was awarded the Nobel Prize in Physics, the Max Planck Medal, the Hughes Medal, the Franklin Medal, the Matteucci Medal, and the Rumford Prize. He has been referred to as the "Architect of the Nuclear Age."

Carrie Fisher (1956-2016) was an American actress and writer best known for her portrayal of Princess Leia in the *Star Wars* films.

Edward FitzGerald (1809-1883) was an English poet and writer best known for the first English translation of The Rubaiyat of Omar Khayyam.

Henry Fonda (1905-1982) was a highly popular American film and stage actor. He appeared in such classic films as *The Grapes of Wrath*, *The Ox-Bow Incident*, *Mister Roberts*, and *12 Angry Men*.

Betty Friedan (1921-2006) was an American writer and feminist icon. Her 1963 book, *The Feminine Mystique*, is generally considered to have galvanized American feminism's second wave in the 20th century.

Milton Friedman (1912-2006) was an American economist and writer who won the Nobel Prize in Economics in 1976 for his research on consumption analysis and monetary history and theory. He was an outspoken advocate for free-market capitalism with a minimum of government intervention.

Frederick James Furnivall (1825-1910) was a British philologist and one of the New English Dictionary's co-creators.

Neil Gaiman (born 1960) is a British author of short fiction, novels, comic books, and films.

Bill Gates (born 1955) is an American billionaire and co-founder of the Microsoft Corporation. He is also one of the leading philanthropists in the world.

Maxim Gorky (1868-1936) was a Russian author credited with bringing Socialist Realism to literature.

Matt Groening (born 1954) is an American cartoonist, producer, and animator who created the popular animated TV series *The Simpsons, Futurama,* and *Disenchantment.*

Stephen Jay Gould (1941-2002) was an American paleontologist, evolutionary biologist, and science historian. His most significant contribution to evolutionary biology was the theory of punctuated equilibrium.

Thomas Hardy (1840-1928) was a noted English novelist and poet.

Neil Patrick Harris (born 1973) is an American actor, writer, and producer best known for his comedy roles on television.

Sadegh Hedayat (1903-1951) was an Iranian writer and novelist.

Robert A. Heinlein (1907-1988) was an American science fiction writer, aeronautical engineer, and retired naval officer referred to as the "dean of science fiction writers."

Joseph Heller (1923-1999) was an American novelist and short-story writer. He is best known for his satirical novel, *Catch 22*.

Alexander Herzen (1812-1870) was a Russian writer and political theorist known as the "father of Russian socialism."

James Hetfield (born 1963) is an American lead singer, guitarist, and co-founder of the wildly popular heavy metal band *Metallica*.

Edwin Hubble (1889-1953) was an American astronomer who played a significant role in establishing extragalactic and obser-vational cosmology. He is regarded as one of the most important astronomers of all time. Most people recognize the Hubble Space Telescope, named in his honor.

David Hume (1711-1776) was a philosopher, historian, and econo-mist. He is considered one of the most influential figures in Western philosophy's history.

Aldous Huxley (1894-1963) was an English novelist, best noted for his classic work *Brave New World*.

Robert G. Ingersoll (1833-1899) was an American lawyer, Civil War veteran, and orator.

A.J. Jacobs (born 1968) is an American journalist, author, and lecturer known for writing about his lifestyle experiments described as immersion journalism.

Angelina Jolie (born 1975) is an American actress, filmmaker, and humanitarian who has received an Academy Award and three Golden Globe awards.

James Joyce (1882-1941) was an influential Irish novelist and poet, best known for his works, *Portrait of The Artist as a Young Man* and *Ulysses*.

Franz Kafka (1883-1924) was a Czech-born Jewish writer best known for his two major works, *The Trial* and *The Metamorphosis*.

Immanuel Kant (1724-1804) was a brilliant German philosopher best known for his monumental work *Critique of Pure Reason*.

John Keats (1795-1821) was an English Romantic poet and one of the most important figures of the second generation of Romantic poets.

Gene Kelly (1912-1996) was an American dancer, singer, film director, and producer noted for the film *Singin' In the Rain*.

John Maynard Keynes (1883-1946) was a British economist whose ideas radically altered the theory and practice of macroeconomics and government's economic policy decisions. He was one of the most influential economists of the 20th century; his ideas served as the basis for Keynesian economics. He detailed these ideas in his monumental work, *The General Theory of Employment, Interest, and Money*, published in 1936.

Larry King (born 1933) is a television talk show host who started *Larry King Live.*

Janusz Korczak (1878-1942) was a Polish-Jewish educator and children's author.

Thomas Kuhn (1922-1996) was an American philosopher of science whose controversial 1962 book, *The Structure of Scientific Revolutions,* significantly impacted academic circles. He introduced the term "paradigm shift," which has since become widely used.

Cloris Leachman (born 1926) is an American actress and comedian who has won eight Primetime Emmy Awards, a Daytime Emmy Award, and an Academy Award for her performance in *The Last Picture Show.*

Stan Lee (1922-2018) was an American comic book writer, editor, producer, and publisher. He was the president and chairman of Marvel Comics.

Stanislaw Lem (1921-2006) was a Polish writer of science fiction and essays on philosophy, futurology, and literary criticism.

Daniel Day-Lewis (born 1957) is a retired British actor who won three Academy Awards for Best Actor—the only male actor to have done so. His award-winning performances were in *My Left Foot, There Will Be Blood,* and *Lincoln.*

H.P. Lovecraft (1890-1937) was an American writer of fictional horror stories. Although he was virtually unknown during his lifetime and died in poverty, he is now considered to be among the most significant 20th-century authors of horror and weird fiction.

Lucretius (99 BC-56 BC) was a Roman poet and philosopher.

Gustav Mahler (1860-1911) was an Austrian composer and one of the leading conductors of his generation.

Bernard Malamud (1914-1986) was a noted Jewish-American author of novels and short stories.

Thomas Mann (1875-1955) was a German novelist, short story writer, and social critic who received the 1929 Nobel Prize in Literature.

Brian May (born 1947) is a British musician and astrophysicist best known as the guitarist for the rock band *Queen*.

Paul McCartney (born 1942) is a British singer, composer, and founding member of the hugely popular rock band *The Beatles*.

H.L. Mencken (1880-1956) was a German American satirist, social critic, and freethinker. He was known as the "Sage of Baltimore."

Francois Mitterrand (1916-1996) served as the president of France from 1981 until 1995.

Edvard Munch (1863-1944) was a Norwegian painter best known for his work *The Scream*.

Elon Musk (born 1971) is an American inventor and entrepreneur from South Africa who is best known for founding SpaceX and cofounding Tesla Motors and PayPal.

Vladimir Nabokov (1899-1977) was a Russian novelist and poet best known for his novel *Lolita*.

John von Neumann (1903-1957) was a Hungarian-American mathematician, physicist, and computer scientist. He was one of the foremost mathematicians of his era, a genius who was comfortable dealing with both pure and applied sciences.

Larry Niven (born 1938) is an American science fiction writer.

Bill Nye (born 1955) is an American science communicator, popular television host, and mechanical engineer. He is widely known as the host of the PBS syndicated children's show, *Bill Nye the Science Guy*.

Eugene O'Neill (1888-1953) was a well-known American playwright who was awarded the Nobel Prize in Literature in 1963. His drama, *Long Day's Journey into Night,* is considered one of the finest American plays of the 20th century.

Sean Penn (born 1960) is an American actor who was twice awarded an Academy Award for Best Actor for his roles in the mystery drama *Mystic River* and the biographical film *Milk*.

Neil Peart (born 1952-2020) was a Canadian author and musician who performed as drummer and lyricist with the rock band *Rush*.

Fernando Pessoa (1888-1935) was a Portuguese poet, writer, literary critic, translator, publisher, and philosopher. He was one of the greatest poets in the Portuguese language.

Brad Pitt (born 1963) is an American actor and film producer. Some of his films include *The Fight Club, Fury,* and *Seven*.

Protagoras (died 420 BC) was an ancient Greek philosopher who stated that Gods' existence was unknowable to the human mind.

Marcel Proust (1871-1922) was a French novelist and critic best known for his work *In Search of Lost Time*.

Phillip Pullman (born 1946) is a British novelist who is the author of several best-selling books.

Alexander Pushkin (1799-1837) was a Russian poet, playwright, and novelist of the Romantic era. He was one of the greatest Russian poets as well as the founder of modern Russian literature.

Andy Rooney (1919-2011) was an American television personality best remembered for his entertaining segment on *60 Minutes*.

Edward Said (1935-2003) was a Palestinian-American literary theorist and advocate for Palestinian rights.

Arthur M. Schlesinger Jr. (1917-2007) was an American historian who was awarded the Pulitzer Prize in 1966 for his book *A Thousand Days: John F. Kennedy in the White House*.

Bertrand Russell (1872-1970) was a British philosopher, mathematician, historian, and political activist. He received the Nobel Prize in Literature in 1950.

Ridley Scott (born 1937) is a British film director and producer. His films include *Alien* and *Blade Runner*.

Mary Shelley (1797-1851) was an English novelist and essayist best known for her Gothic horror novel *Frankenstein*, published in 1818.

Edward Snowden (born 1983) is an American computer specialist, privacy activist, and former CIA employee and NSA contractor accused of disclosing classified information regarding top-secret US and British government surveillance programs.

Herbert Spencer (1820-1903) was a British philosopher, biologist, anthropologist, and sociologist. He coined the term "survival of the fittest," which he used in *Principles of Biology*, published in 1864.

Elizabeth Cady Stanton (1815-1902) was an American social activist and abolitionist.

Olaf Stapledon (1886-1950) was a British philosopher and author of science fiction.

John Steinbeck (1902-1968) was an American writer best known for his novels *The Grapes of Wrath, Of Mice and Men,* and *East of Eden.* He received the Nobel Prize in Literature in 1962.

Howard Stern (born 1954) is an American radio and television personality, producer, author, and actor.

Sting (also known as Gordon Matthew Thomas Sumner, born 1951) is an English musician and actor who became famous with the new wave rock band T*he Police* in the late 70s.

Boris Strugatsky (1925-2012) was a Soviet-Russian science fiction writer who collaborated with his brother Arkady on several works.

Edward Teller (1908-2003) was a Hungarian-American theoretical physicist known as "the father of the hydrogen bomb," a title which he did not care for in the least. He was a member of the Manhattan Project, which developed the first atomic bomb. His contributions to the field of theoretical physics are numerous.

Charles Templeton (1915-2001) was a Canadian cartoonist, evangelist, politician, newspaper editor, inventor, broadcaster, and author.

Thucydides (c.460-c.395 BC) was a Greek historian and author who wrote *History of the Peloponnesian War*, which recounts the 5th-century war between Sparta and Athens. He has been labeled the father of scientific history due to his strict methodology of gathering evidence in terms of cause and effect without reference to Gods' intervention.

Ivan Turgenev (1818-1883) was a Russian novelist, poet, playwright, and translator.

Mary Wollstonecraft (1759-1797) was a British writer, philosopher, and advocate of women's rights.

Ted Turner (born 1938) is an American media mogul who founded the Cable News Network. He is also a noted philanthropist who donated one billion dollars to the United Nations, which created the United Nations Foundation.

Mark Twain (1835-1910) was an American humorist, public speaker, and writer. He wrote the famous novels *Adventures of Huckleberry Finn* and *The Adventures of Tom Sawyer*.

Neil deGrasse Tyson (born 1958) is an American astrophysicist, author, and television personality. He has been the Frederick P. Rose Director of the Hayden Planetarium at the Rose Center for Earth and Space in New York City since 1996. Some of his books include *Death by Black Hole, Astrophysics for People in a Hurry*, and *Merlin's Tour of the Universe*.

Giuseppe Verdi (1813-1901) was an influential Italian composer during the 19th century. His works include *La Traviata* and *Aida*.

Voltaire or François-Marie Arouet (1694-1778) was a French philosopher, writer, and historian during the Enlightenment period. He was critical of organized religion, particularly the Roman Catholic Church. Voltaire may have been a deist rather than an agnostic, perhaps believing in a God who is aloof and utterly unconcerned about humanity's affairs.

Elie Wiesel (1928-2016) was a Jewish-American writer, political activist, professor, and Holocaust survivor originally from Romania. He was the author of fifty-seven books and received the Nobel Peace Prize in 1986.

Ludwig Wittgenstein (1889-1951) was an Austrian philosopher who worked primarily in logic, mathematics, and the philosophy of mind and language. Some regard him as one of the most influential philosophers of the twentieth century. He served as a professor at the University of Cambridge from 1929 to 1947.

Steve Wozniak (born 1950) is an American inventor, electronics engineer, programmer, philanthropist, and technology entrepreneur. In 1976, he co-founded Apple Inc., which later became the world's largest information technology company. Many regard him and co-founder Steve Jobs as the foremost pioneers of the personal computer revolution of the 1970s and 1980s.

Émile Zola (1840-1902) was an influential French writer and contributor to the development of theatrical naturalism.

AUTHOR BIO

Robert K. Cooper is a 68-year-old author living in the Dallas, Texas area. Robert has an undergraduate degree in Economics and a Master's degree in Sociology. He worked for twenty years in corporate information technology and fifteen years as a licensed real estate appraiser. His hobbies include reading, music, and internet chess.

Please feel free to post a review of the
book on your favorite retail site.

DEDICATION

To my adopted parents who did the best they could for me in this random, perplexing world.

ENDNOTES

1   Schiappa, E. (2003). *Protagoras and Logos: A Study in Greek Philosophy and Rhetoric.* Columbia, South Carolina: University of South Carolina Press.

2   Huxley, T. H. (1992). *Agnosticism and Christianity, and other essays.* Buffalo, N.Y: Prometheus Books.

3   Russell, Bertrand. (1957). *Why I Am Not a Christian: And Other Essays on Religion and Related Subjects.* New York, New York: Simon & Schuster, Inc.

4   Dikotter, Frank. (2010). *Mao's Great Famine: The History of China's Most Devastating Catastrophe, 1958-1962.* New York, New York: Walker Publishing Company, Inc.

5   Pye, Lucian W. (1996). "Reassessing the Cultural Revolution." *The China Quarterly. 108:* 597-612.

6   Conquest, Robert. *The Great Terror: A Reassessment.* Fortieth Anniversary Ed. Oxford and New York: Oxford University Press. 2008.

7   Khlevniuk, O. & Favorov, N. *Stalin: New Biography of a Dictator.* New Haven: Yale University Press. 2015.

8   Toland, J. (1992). *Adolf Hitler.* New York: Anchor Books.

9   Chandler, David P. *Brother Number One. A Political Biography of Pol Pot.* Boulder, San Francisco, and Oxford: Westview Press. 1992.

10   Thoughtco. "Biography of Idi Amin, Brutal Dictator of Uganda." *Thoughtco,* Updated 13 May 2019

11   Eckstein, S. (2003). *Back from the future: Cuba under Castro.* New York, NY: Routledge.

12   Karsh, E. & Rautsi, I. (2002). *Saddam Hussein: a political biography.* New York: Grove Press.

13   The Editors of Encyclopedia Britannica. "Muammar Al-Qaddafi." *Encyclopedia Britannica,* Encyclopedia Britannica, Inc., 16 Oct. 2019.

14   Memmott, Mark. "Flashback: Reagan Calls Gadhafi the 'Mad
     Dog Of The Middle East'." *NPR*, NPR, 22 Feb. 2011.

15   The Editors of Encyclopedia Britannica. "Muammar
     Al-Qaddafi." *Encyclopedia Britannica*, Encyclopedia
     Britannica, Inc., 16 Oct. 2019.

16   "Opening the Hermit Kingdom." *History Today*.

17   "Kim Jong-Un." *Biography.com*, A&E Networks Television, 9 July 2019.

18   Stevens, Matt. "Trump and Kim Jong-Un, and the Names They've Called
     Each Other." *The New York Times*, The New York Times, 9 Mar. 2018.

19   *The Galveston hurricane of 1900: the deadliest natural disaster in
     American history*. United States Lexington, KY: Charles River Publishers.

20   *Hearn, Phillip (2004). Hurricane Camille: Monster Storm
     of the Gulf Coast. University Press of Mississippi.*

21   Brown, D. (2015). *Drowned City: Hurricane Katrina & New
     Orleans*. New York, NY: Houghton Mifflin Harcourt.

22   (2019). *Weather.gov*.

23   Felix, R. (2018). *Hurricane Harvey: disaster in Texas and
     beyond*. Minneapolis, Minnesota: Millbrook Press.

24   Lynch, J. (2017). *2017 Atlantic Hurricane Season in Review: One for the
     Record Books | Improving public understanding of insurance. Iii.org.*

25   Masters, J. (2018). *An Active and Destructive 2018 Atlantic
     Hurricane Season Ends*. Weather Underground.

26   *World Fire Statistics | CTIF - International Association of Fire
     Services for Safer Citizens through Skilled Firefighters*. (2019).

27   Fimrite, P., & Cabanatuan, M. (2018). *Mendocino Complex blaze
     is now largest wildfire in California history*. SFChronicle.com.

28   *Why the Carr Fire in Northern California is so severe*. (2018). Vox.

29   *NPR Choice page. California's Camp Fire Becomes
     the Deadliest in State History*. (2018).

30   *Tally of buildings destroyed in Woolsey fire tops 1,500*. (2018). *Curbed LA*.

31   Finnegan, W. (2018). *California Burning. The New York Review of Books*.

32 Paddison, Laura. "2019 Was the Year The World Burned | HuffPost." *Huffpost.*, 27 Dec 2019

33 Frank, Thomas. "Climate Impacts: Wildfires Plummeted in 2019. Experts Say It Won't Last. ClimateWire. 18 Mar 2020.

34 "Japan Earthquake & Tsunami of 2011: Facts and Information." *LiveScience.*

35 Pletcher, Kenneth, and John P. Rafferty. "Japan Earthquake and Tsunami of 2011." *Encyclopedia Britannica*, Encyclopedia Britannica. 4 Mar. 2019.

36 Pletcher, Kenneth, and John P. Rafferty. "Sichuan Earthquake of 2008." *Encyclopedia Britannica*, Encyclopedia Britannica 5 May 2019.

37 Watts, Jonathan. "Sichuan Quake: China's Earthquake Reconstruction to Cost $150bn." *The Guardian*, Guardian News and Media, 14 Aug. 2008.

38 "2008- Cyclone Nargis." *Hurricanes*.hurricanescience. org/history/storms/2000s/cyclonenargis/.

39 The Editors of Encyclopedia Britannica. "Indian Ocean Tsunami of 2004." *Encyclopedia Britannica*, Encyclopedia Britannica 13 Mar. 2019

40 Natsios, Andrew S. *The Great North Korean Famine:* United States Institute of Peace Press, 2001.

41 Taubenberger, Jeffery K, and David M Morens. "1918 Influenza: The Mother of All Pandemics." *Emerging Infectious Diseases*, Centers for Disease Control and Prevention, Jan. 2006.

42 Martini, M, et al. "The Spanish Influenza Pandemic: a Lesson from History 100 Years after 1918." *Journal of Preventive Medicine and Hygiene*, Pacini Editore Srl, 29 Mar. 2019.

43 Arnold, Catharine [VNV]. *Pandemic 1918: The Story of the Deadliest Influenza in History*. Michael OMara Books Limited, 2018.

44 Halsey, Ashley. "The Flu Can Kill Tens of Millions of People. In 1918, That's Exactly What It Did." *The Washington Post*, WP Company, 1 Apr. 2019.

45 Suhone, L., Tennoe, M., & Henssonow, S. (2010). *1920 Haiyuan Earthquake*. Betascript Publishing

46 Palmer, J. (2012). *Heaven cracks, earth shakes: the Tangshan Earthquake and the death of Mao's China*. New York: Basic Books, a member of the Perseus Books Group.

47   Sensarma, A. (1995). The Great Bengal Cyclone of 1737 – an enquiry into the legend. *Current Science, 68*(1), 114-117. Retrieved from http://www.jstor.org/stable/24096184

48   *Hurricanes: Science and Society: 1839- Coringa Cyclone.* (2019). *Hurricanescience.org.* Retrieved from http://www.hurricanescience.org/history/storms/pre1900s/1839/

49   Benoit, P. (2012). *The Haitian earthquake of 2010.* New York: Children's Press.

50   Rohde, C. (2014). *Catalyst: In the Wake of the Great Bhola Cyclone.* CreateSpace Independent Publishing Platform

51   Soda, I. (2016). *1556 Shaanxi Earthquake: Deadliest Earthquake in History - Fancy Frindle.*

52   1887, Y. (1887). *Yellow River Flood of 1887. World History Project.*

53   Courtney, C. (2018). *The nature of disaster in China: the 1931 Yangzi River flood.* Cambridge, United Kingdom: Cambridge University Press.

54   Harris, L. (2018). *The Peking gazette: a reader in nineteenth-century Chinese history.* Leiden Boston: Brill.

55   Wallenfeldt, Jeff. "Texas Tower Shooting of 1966." *Encyclopedia Britannica*, Encyclopedia Britannica 25 July 2019.

56   Tawnell D. Hobbs, K. (2019). *Mass Shootings in El Paso, Dayton Leave 31 Dead. WSJ.*

57   *Dayton Gunman Had Been Exploring 'Violent Ideologies,' F.B.I. Says.* (2019). *Nytimes.com.*

58   Garrison, J. (2019). *What We Know About the Suspect in the Virginia Beach Shooting That Killed 12.* [online] Usatoday.com.

59   Coutu, Peter. "Gunman emailed resignation hours before killing 12 people in Virginia Beach's deadliest shooting." (2019). *Virginian-Pilot.*

60   *New Zealand terrorist attack leaves 49 dead, more than 40 injured.* (2019). *South China Morning Post.*

61   *Christchurch Mosque Shootings Were Partly Streamed on Facebook.* (2019). *Nytimes.com.*

62   Fauria, K. and Cooper, J. (2019). *Marine combat veteran kills 12 in rampage at California bar.* [online] AP NEWS.

63   Karlamangla, S. (2018). *Mental health experts declined to commit Thousand Oaks gunman Ian David Long after April disturbance.* [online] latimes.com.

64   Robertson, C., Mele, C. and Tavernise, S. (2018). *11 Killed in Synagogue Massacre; Suspect Charged With 29 Counts.* [online] Nytimes.com.

65   Roth, Andrew. "Crimea College Attack: Student Carries Out Mass Shooting in Kerch." *The Guardian.* 17 Oct 2018.

66   Kravtsova, Irina. "How Were We Supposed to Know What Was in His Head? Life in Kerch, a Day After A School Massacre Rocked the City." *Meduza.* Translated by Rothrock, Kevin. 19 Oct 2018.

67   Joyce, Kathleen. "Texas High School Shooting Leaves at Least 8 Dead, Suspect in Custody." *Fox News.* 18 May 2018

68   Abc13. "Santa Fe HS shooting suspect Dimitrios Pagourtzis moved to state mental hospital - ABC13 Houston." *Abc13,* 06 Dec 2019.

69   Brown, J. (2017, February 17). *To Longtime Friend, School Shooter Nikolas Cruz was Lonely, Volatile, Ostracized.* Miami Herald.

70   *Devin Patrick Kelley: What we know about the Texas church shooting suspect.* (2017). *Cbsnews.com.* /

71   *NPR Choice page. Texas Church Shooter May Have Been Motivated to Kill by Domestic Situation.* (2019). *Npr.org.*

72   Stevens, J. (2017). *The Las Vegas Massacre: Stephen Paddock and the 2017 Las Vegas Shooting.* CreateSpace Independent Publishing Platform

73   Lavandera, Ed. "How the Dallas Massacre Unfolded." *CNN.* 20 Jul 2016

74   Associated Press. "Dallas Sniper Profile: Micah Johnson was sent home from Afghanistan | US news | The Guardian." *Theguardian,* 09 Jul 2016

75   Damian Paletta, A. *A Life of Violent Threats Paved Way for Orlando Attack. WSJ.*

76   *What We Know About the Suspected Orlando Nightclub Shooter. ABC News.*

77   Saeed Ahmed and Ralph Ellis, C. (2019). *Mass shooting at Inland Regional Center: What we know - CNN. CNN.*

78   Winston, R. (2016). *A year after the San Bernardino terror attack, the FBI is still struggling to answer key questions.* [online] latimes.com.

79   Marszal, A. (2015). *Dylann Roof confesses to Charleston shooting as governor calls for death penalty. Telegraph.co.uk.*

80   *Sandy Hook Shooter Adam Lanza's Spreadsheet Detailing Centuries of Mass Violence Served as a Roadmap to Murder.* (2018). *Courant.com.*

81   Griffin, A., & Kovner, J. (2013). A Chilling Look into Adam Lanza's World. *Hartford Courant.*

82   Reid, W. (2018). *A dark night in Aurora: inside James Holmes and the Colorado mass shootings.* New York, NY: Skyhorse Publishing.

83   *Aurora theater shooter James Holmes psychiatric reports unsealed by 2015 trial Judge Carlos Samour.* (2019). *Denverpost.com.*

84   Turrettini, U. & Puckett, K. (2017). *The mystery of the lone wolf killer: Anders Behring Breivik and the threat of terror in plain sight.* New York, NY: Pegasus Crime.

85   Seierstad, A. & Death, S. (2015). *One of us: the story of Anders Breivik and the massacre in Norway.* New York: Farrar, Straus & Giroux.

86   Archives. "FBI — Jared Lee Loughner Sentenced in Arizona on Federal Charges in Tucson Shooting." *Archives.* 08 Nov 2012.

87   BBC. "Profile: Arizona shooting suspect Jared Loughner - BBC News." *BBC.* 11 Jan 2011.

88   McGarry, B. (2019). *New Documentary Explores What Drove Fort Hood Shooter to Extremism. Military.com.*

89   Yang, W (2011). *The Face of Seung-Hui Cho.* n+1 Foundation, Inc.

90   Bovsun, M. (2015). *Mystery Still Surrounds Charles Carl Roberts' 2006 Murderous Rampage in West Nickels Mine.* NY Daily News.

91   Sevcik, K. (2005). *Reservation for death.* Salon.

92   Erfurt, T. (2002). *Double life of massacre gunman. Telegraph.co.uk.*

93   Toppo, Greg. "10 Years Later, The Real Story Behind Columbine." *usatoday.com,* 13 Apr 2009

94   Cullen, D. (2009). *Columbine.* New York: Twelve

95   Affidavit: Columbine shooter posted threat on Web. Cnn.com. 10 Apr 2001.

96 Rcfp. "District attorney releases Columbine gunman's juvenile records - The Reporters Committee for Freedom of the Press." *Rcfp*. 06 Nov 2002.

97 Cullen, Dave. "Columbine." 03 Mar 2010. Print.